BIRDING TIMES, A LIFE IN RHYMES

By
Lynn E. Barber

Thank you, Dave

for being part of my life for over 57 years,

and for putting up with, and

even sometimes encouraging

my birding and

my rhyme writing.

Copyright 2024

by Lynn E. Barber

All rights reserved

First edition

TABLE OF CONTENTS

Preface v
Introduction vi
BIRDING AND RHYMING – A LIFETIME JOURNEY 1
   Autobiographical Accounts 1
   Childhood Writing 14
   Special Birds and Other Critters, As I Was Growing Up 22
   Thoughts on Being a Birder in a Non-Birding Family 35
   Keeping Bird Lists 36
RHYMING THROUGH THE YEARS 39
   Rhyming 39
   Rhymes Written over almost 21 Years in North Carolina (1979-2000) 45
   Rhymes Written in and around Texas (Not Big Year Poems) (2001-2010) 53
   Rhymes about Alaska Birding (2000 and 2014-2022) 61
   Rhymes about Wisconsin Birding and More after Returning to Wisconsin (May 2021 to the Present) 67
HARDCORE BIRDING TIMES AND RHYMES 88
   Travels with Lynn 88
   Summary of Earlier Travels – 1979-1996 88
   1992 - Costa Rica 89
   1993 – Venezuela 90
   1994 – Kenya and the Galapagos Islands 91
   1997 - Bhutan (and India) 92
   1998 – Antarctica 98
   1999 - Finland 101
   1999 – Midway Island 104
   2000 - Israel and Jordan 104

2001 - The Philippines	105
2002 - Peru	112
2002- California & Arizona	113
2002– Cuba	115
2002 – Sichuan China	116
2003 - Ecuador	120
2013 – Honduras	122
Pelagic Trips	122
Big Year Years	127
Texas (2003 and 2005)	130
Obsessing about Doing (and Doing) an ABA Big Year (2006-2008)	138
Alaska Big Year (2016)	152
Wisconsin Big Year (2022) and More	153
To Chase or Not to Chase	156
Hummingbirds	160
OTHER TIMES, MORE LIFE, MORE RHYMES	**166**
Volunteering (Non-church and Non-bird Related)	166
Churchy Stuff	174
One Must Work	183
Dave and Marriage	191
Angst, Questions and Inspiration	195
Death and Dying	228
Dogs	247
Poems to Order	249
(On Being Asked to Write Poems)	249
Pandemic Poetry	254
Fiction/Stories	256
Very Miscellaneous	259

INDEX 262

Preface

It Matters (9/17/22)

Someone recently said (in a sermon, I recall),
What we do does matter, but it huge or be it small.
Even standing still, with the world around us churning
Becomes a kind of doing, a candle brightly burning.
A quiet voice of witness, a gentle word of peace,
A holding back of anger, when hurtful deeds can cease.
Actions not dramatic, nor glorious or bold,
But actions to inspire, and wondrous to behold.

Like most people who write about themselves, I feel a need to tell others about where I have been, what I have thought, and what matters to me. I have no unfounded belief that this telling will be "wondrous" to others or will inspire them, but I hope that my journey, and possibly some of my thoughts, will have some meaning to someone besides me.

INTRODUCTION

As will become evident throughout this book, I am a birder and a writer of rhyming poetry. I also am a bird photographer and a painter of birds. For most of the years of my life, since I was about seven, my life has revolved around birds. This book includes accounts of birding and other highlights throughout my life interwoven with poems that I have written about a wide variety of topics, interspersed with a few sketches and black-and-white copies of some of my acrylic paintings. Although I have written so many poems, there are large parts of my life that have occurred without any attempt to write poems, so this book also includes prose to fill in some of the blanks as well as to explain or give background for at least some of the more cryptic poems. There have also been mostly forgotten parts of my life where birds have not been central and where no poems were written.

Organizing this book was more difficult than I first imagined. Should it be chronological, year by year, with poems on a great diversity of topics sprinkled along when they were written? Or should it be by topic, such as poems and prose about my life story, on birding adventures, on the need to write poems, etc. I finally decided to do it topic by topic. That mostly worked except, of course, there were quite a few poems on multiple topics, so I had to decide on the section in which to include them. Then I had to figure out some kind of logical (at least to me) sequence for the topics.

The autobiographical first section, after a concise 5-year by 5-year summary of my life so far, comprises a mostly prose overview of my life, beginning with an excerpt written when I was a child, followed by an update written as an adult, also mostly in prose. Following that are sections on rhyming and on bird-related topics, and also non-bird poems written throughout my life. These later sections are primarily in rhyme, with explanations in prose where it seemed they might clarify the rhymes.

I also need to say a few words about the poems that I have included in this book. If I know when the poems were written that date appears in parentheses after the title of the poem. Sometimes I have made an educated guess as to the likely time when they were written. I have organized the poems into sections, generally related to the poems' topics. Within each section I have put the poems in chronological order. Although I prefer not to use footnotes, where the poem appears to me to require some explanation, I have added it either just before the poem or in a footnote immediately after the poem. I have sometimes edited my poems for this book to correct or clarify them as seems to make sense to me now. Sometimes I originally included titles when I wrote a poem, or they may have been added later to help give the reader a clue as to where or why they were written or what they are about.

I noticed as I reviewed the rhymes in this book (as you will see), that in many of my rhymes over the years I have found it necessary or convenient to rhyme "words" with "birds." It makes sense to me – these two things have governed much of my life. Hopefully, the regular use of this rhyme pairing will just serve to emphasize the importance of these topics to me, rather than detracting from the meanings of the poems.

Finally, I wish to thank everyone who has been part of my birding and rhyming existence and experience – way too many people to even begin to name. Thank you!

BIRDING AND RHYMING – A LIFETIME JOURNEY

Autobiographical Accounts

Autobiography? (8/2/21)

A book about me? Don't be absurd!
A book about me? They'll not read a word!
But maybe *you* will?

The following concise chronology is an outline of my life (so far), in 5-year increments so you can see the overall picture of where I've been and what I've done, extremely encapsulated. Following this outline, I have expanded on my earliest years, including a few paragraphs written when I was seven years old.

Autobiographical sketch

Summary of what was happening in my life:

- (1946-51) Age 0-5: a baby and child in Wausau and then in Schofield, WI. While I do remember a few things that occurred then, mostly I have hand-me-down stories of what life was like.

- (1952-56) Age 6-10: we moved to our Mosinee (WI) farm, and I discovered birds.

- (1957-61) Age 11-15: the awkward, love-to-bird-but-don't-tell-anyone, junior high and high school years (D.C. Everest High School, Schofield).

- (1962-66) Age 15-20: finish high school, begin college and major in zoology at the UW Madison.

- (1967-71) Age 21-25: meet and marry Dave Barber, graduate from college with a BA in zoology and Dave with a MS in meteorology; we move to AK for a year.

- (1972-76) Age 26-30: start grad school in bacteriology at the UW Madison, earn MS and PhD in bacteriology and Dave earns PhD in meteorology; we move to Corvallis, OR.

- (1977-81) Age 31-35: travel to Mexico and Sweden for work; change jobs in OR; move to Raleigh, NC and become Research Microbiologist with the USDA at NCSU; Dave becomes meteorology professor at NCSU; join Community United Church of Christ (UCC).

- (1982-86) Age 36-40: become inspired to go to law school; go to law school at Duke University, become patent attorney upon receiving JD degree; Dave goes to divinity school, also at Duke.

- (1987-91) Age 41-45: change law firms, learn to love patent lawyering at Olive & Olive in Durham, busy with activities of all kinds (ACLU, Human Rights, Audubon, Carolina Bird Club); Dave receives MDiv degree and becomes pastor at Community UCC.

- (1992-96) Age 46-50: international bird traveling begins in Costa Rica, begin to yearn for autonomy from law firm and make a list of pros and cons on whether to leave; mother dies of cancer; start my own solo patent practice.

- 1997-2001) Age 51-55: traumatic events continue: father dies, I'm executrix, long months of estate stuff; Dave decides to change church jobs and interviews out west; we move to Fort Worth, TX where Dave becomes pastor of First Congregational UCC; I continue in solo patent law practice.

- (2002-06) Age 56-60: still living in TX; increased birding while still in solo practice; do 2 TX big years of birding.

- (2007-11) Age 61-65: do ABA birding big year; write book on it, which is published by Texas A&M University Press (*Extreme Birder: One Woman's Big Year*); Dave retires from being a pastor and goes back into meteorology and begins to work for US Weather Service; we move to Rapid City, SD where he works for the Weather Service; I continue in solo patent practice.

- (2012-16) Age 66-70: we move to Anchorage, AK where Dave becomes a forecaster; I write and publish a book on endangered birds (*Birds in Trouble*) and do an AK big year of birding.

- (2017-21) Age 71-75: write and publish book on comparing AK & TX big years (*Big Years, Biggest States: Birding in Texas and Alaska*); both of us retire; we move to Wausau, WI, explore Marathon County birding; contemplate WI big year.

- (2022-2024) Age 76-78: Do one WI big year and another less big, big year; begin writing and submit book to publisher about owls of the US and Canada and beyond (running title: *A Charisma of Owls*); finish painting pictures of all of these owls plus other owls plus two possible covers for owl book; become VP of Wisconsin Society for Ornithology and then President, and then *finally* pick up this "rhyme book" manuscript draft from where it has languished for a few years to revise and update it for possible publishing.

As a Child-what my life was like as birding and rhyming took over (written when I was about 7 years old and edited slightly for accuracy and completeness; my name then was Lynn Eileen Sternberg).

I was born in Wausau at Memorial Hospital on May 17, 1946. I lived there [in Wausau, not at the hospital] for two years. I was always mischievous and always got into trouble. When I first saw snow, I asked Mommy, "Why is it raining suds?" Once when my father was mixing paint, I stepped into a pail full of it. I was really a mess! I called all objects shaped like pens, "pints". One day when I was coming down the stairs, I saw some of Daddy's big bolts. Happily, I started playing with Daddy's "pints".

My sister [Ann] was born in Wausau, too. When I was two years old, we moved to Schofield, where we lived across from the Drive-In Theater. While we lived there, we owned a few ducks and mink. It was always fun to watch the horses too, although we were too young to ride them and stay on.

Then I started school. It was at Schofield School that I went to kindergarten and first grade. My kindergarten teacher was Mrs. Cuff, and my first-grade teacher was Mrs. Aldridge. While I was in kindergarten I had a broken arm, chicken pox and measles. I wasn't in school very much that year.

When I was in kindergarten, we moved to Route #2, Mosinee. We lived in a big old white house which was surrounded by farm buildings. The first year we only had a few chickens, but the second year we had 500 of them. It was a big job to feed them all.

Why Bird? Another Autobiographical Account

The first part below was originally written in 2011. It was subsequently revised and updated.

This section, among other things, attempts to answer the question, "Why did I become a birder and what is it that makes me go birding?" On a drive from Raleigh west to the North Carolina mountains for a folk-dance weekend sometime in the 90s, a non-birding friend asked me this question, and I was stumped. Was it due to where I grew up? Of course, I had no choice where I was born – central Wisconsin. My parents (Carl and Ruth Sternberg) both grew up there, met there, married there, had two children there, and lived the rest of their lives in Marathon County in the center of the state. But they did not become birders. Maybe the answer to this question is hidden in my poems (or is obvious there).

I lived in Wisconsin until I was married in my early 20s. Although my parents spent their entire lives there, I have lived in six states since then, with my birding passion growing, growing. As discussed in more detail below, in brief, my life has taken me from the upper Midwest (Wisconsin) to Alaska in 1968, back to WI in 1969, to Corvallis, Oregon in 1974, to Raleigh, North Carolina in 1979, to Fort Worth, Texas in 2000, back to the western upper Midwest (Rapid City, South Dakota) in 2010, back to Alaska in 2014 and back to Wisconsin in 2021.

Thinking back to over seven decades ago, the first houses of my life are only vaguely remembered. The first house in Wausau in

Marathon County in central Wisconsin, was a large downtown house that I understand became a funeral home after my parents moved from there to our second house, which was side-by-side with my aunt and uncle's house in Schofield. This second house was surrounded by large open fields where horses spent their last days until becoming horsemeat to feed to foxes and mink, some of which were raised by my uncle and my parents. I'm sure there were birds there, but all I remember is the frightening flies that I as a four-year old stared at through the back screen door.

Things improved considerably at our third house, in rural Mosinee, also in Marathon County. For reasons mostly unknown to me, when I was about five and my sister Ann about three, our family all moved out to the country where my parents had bought a 160-acre, probably run-down, farm, which I later realized was a bird-heaven on earth. This is where I discovered birds. I sometimes think that it's no wonder I grew up to be a birder.

Our new home was an old farmhouse toward one side of the 160-acre neglected farm. It did not have indoor plumbing – yet – but a handpump on the front porch provided water, and a small wooden building not too far away met the other necessary plumbing requirement. The yard contained a very large red cowbarn, with facilities for having milk cows and a large hay-filled loft. Also, in and around the yard were a machine shed, numerous smaller buildings originally used for chickens and pigs, but now used for chickens and little girls' play places. The yard also had wonderful smelling lilacs, willows and wild black-, pin- and choke-cherry trees.

This land around the farmyard was also a child's paradise of small jack pine clumps surrounded by alfalfa or grassy fields, one larger wooded area visible from the country road, as was the farmhouse. Old grown-over grassy vehicle lanes bordered the fields with clumps of hazel brush and weeds along the fence lines. At the back of the property away from the road was an expanse of wild small deciduous saplings (poplar, birch) and miscellaneous brush, leading to a wandering length of Bull Junior Creek flowing through an area of large, beautiful birch trees. Years later, the opening scenes of *Dr.*

Zhivago (watch it; you'll see) always brought tears of remembrance to my eyes.

Egg prices had been rising steadily about this time, which led my parents to rip out the stanchions in the cowbarn and have a cement floor poured. The barn was then filled with cheeping chicks, which grew to be producers of eggs for sale. Because egg prices fell dramatically at that time (probably because many other people had also gone into the egg-producing business), eggs became a major feature in our diets (breakfast, custard pies, angel food cakes, etc.) as did chicken. As children we learned to help with turning a chicken from a warm-blooded companion to dinner. Looking back, the process seems rather cold-hearted, but then it was accomplished without a second thought.

There were other more friendly, less flighty chickens that were raised in some of the outbuildings and allowed to roam the yard. Many of these became "pets" with such creative names as "Brownback" (had sat below another chicken on the roost on an earlier night) or "Brownwing", etc. Usually, we coped okay with the demise of these too, my mother being careful not to fry and serve chicken from the freezer until our memories of any possible traumas had faded.

My parents, seeing how enamored we were of all the animals, also bought ducklings and goslings every now and then, resulting in a noisy yard and eventually in more baby ducklings. Those we never had for dinner. You have not really lived unless you have (preferably as a child) "fuzzed" a duckling or chick – held a very young bird carefully to your cheek and felt the soft warm tickle of the downy side, back and head of the bird.

A Farmyard Memory (4/9/09, I think) (one of my very few unrhyming poems)

My sister and I, aged nine and eleven,
Lead the parade, giggling, and
Looking back more often than we watch where we're going,
Rattle the cans of cracked corn
In rhythm with our steps across the wide farmyard.
Flapping their wings to keep up with us,
The two long-necked geese honk excitedly.
The eight or so waddling ducks are trying to keep up with the geese.
And at the rear of the parade are the cackling, squawky chickens,
Strong yellow legs striding as fast as they can after the ducks.
We are the pied pipers of Mosinee, Wisconsin,
And very important to the barnyard world.

The main animals on our farm, however, were not chickens or ducks or geese, but mink. The mink were housed individually elevated above the ground in wire cages with straw-filled wooden kennels attached to one end of each cage. We soon learned that these cages and the kennels, when not being used for mink, could also hold a variety of wild critters that I started corralling to bring home (toads, baby birds such as starlings and a crow, 13-lined ground squirrels, and a baby red squirrel rescued from a birdhouse before eviction by my father), or which were caught in one of my father's wild animal traps, including a weasel, a muskrat, and rabbits. Some of the baby mink also became pets until their teeth became too sharp for us to handle them safely.

After the farmhouse was brought up to date by my father on its wiring and on its plumbing and other structural features, my parents sold the farmhouse, built a house-sized cement-block building across the fields from the farmhouse, nestled next to a jack pine-birch wooded area, and moved us and all the remaining animals (mink and ducks; the chicken business had been phased out) across the field. We lived in the often-damp cement building for a number of years until they built a modern ranch house close by, which was built based on my parents' long-held dream designs. My father did essentially all the construction and interior work of both buildings single-handedly, with a little help now and then from the rest of us. The cement block building reverted to its original intended use for storage and mink-ranching activities when we moved out. By the time my family moved into the new house, I had almost finished high school and soon was off to Madison for college.

I spent four years in Madison at the University of Wisconsin working on my BA degree in zoology hoping to eventually become an ornithology professor. I chose a BA and not a BS because in my teenage mind a BS degree almost sounded like swearing. I did nearly all my birdwatching during those years off-campus at the Madison Arboretum.

In the middle of my junior year, I met Dave Barber. We dated nonstop and got married after I completed my work on my bachelor's degree and he on his master's degree. He took a job with the Weather Bureau (now the US Weather Service), which had employed him periodically during college. Knowing my interest in seeing new birds (as, I guess, did everyone I knew), when he learned that the Weather Bureau had a special program to encourage people to take jobs in San Juan, Puerto Rico or in Anchorage, AK, both places with birds I had never seen, he asked me to which of these places I wanted to go. I jumped at the possibility of San Juan – all those wonderful birds would be new. But soon, upon thinking it over, I realized that one reason for all the birds in Puerto Rico was probably all the insects and the year-round muggy weather without a refreshing cool season, and certainly no snow. My fervor cooled and I asked him to apply for Anchorage instead, which he did. Before we were married, he received word that had gotten the Anchorage job. We drove the 4000 miles from Madison to Anchorage the week after we were married in June 1968, in our new-to-us used Econoline Ford van that had been fitted out by a previous owner with a bed, stove and sink.

After a year and a summer in Alaska, we came back to Madison, to become more educated. Dave completed a PhD in meteorology and after a couple of years working in a food microbiology lab, I began and completed a food microbiology MS (*Staphylococcus* spoilage of sausage), and then a PhD in microbial ecology (methane production in lake sediments).

In 1974, with PhD degrees in hand, we drove to Corvallis, Oregon, to begin post-doctoral positions at Oregon State University, his being an assistant professor in the Atmospheric Science department and mine in the Botany and Plant Pathology department doing research on free-living nitrogen-fixing bacteria. A couple of years later I obtained a research position in the Microbiology Department doing research on *Rhizobium meliloti* bacteria that beneficially form nitrogen-fixing nodules on alfalfa plants enabling the plants to grow with less or no added nitrogen fertilizer.

After about four years at Oregon State University, various job-related factors led us to begin to think of looking for jobs elsewhere, anywhere that had some possibility of a job in meteorology and another in microbiology. A few job leads (Hawaii and Oklahoma) did not pan out, but suddenly there appeared a meteorology position at North Carolina State University, and a possible opening with the USDA at NCSU doing more nitrogen-fixation research with *Rhizobium* and legumes. Everything fell into place, and we moved to Raleigh in 1979 and became assistant professors there.

Three years later I became entranced with the idea of changing careers and going into law. My ever-cynical father once said that even though he was not fond of lawyers (as far as I know there were no other lawyers in our family), if somebody was going to be bilking others of their money, he was glad it was going to be his daughter. I had not even been aware of the field of patent law when I went to law school, much less had I considered it, but it turned out that only those relatively rare people with both a law degree and a degree in science or engineering were qualified to take the federal patent exam to become patent attorneys (if they passed a state bar exam and also the US government's patent exam). In my 3rd year in law school, I started being contacted by law firms wondering if I might be interested in joining their firm as a patent attorney when I graduated. I worked for the next summer at a small local Research Triangle Park firm that ultimately flew me to NY for a patent law crash course (law schools don't get into the necessary weeds on the topic) and then hired me as their new patent attorney.

We decided to move from our original new home in Raleigh to a less expensive house to help us to afford our continued education (my law degree and later, Dave's MDiv degree). Instead of living in our brand-new multi-level, high ceilinged place in a new subdivision where we had first lived in Raleigh, we moved into an old house in an old Raleigh neighborhood. The old house did not have much of a window view, but it did have lush vegetation that threatened to take over the yard in the muggy, hot climate.

Although I worked as a patent attorney at law firms for a while (10 years at two different firms), the realization that I might be able to go out on my own as a solo lawyer and have increased freedom to periodically choose to go birding instead of write patent applications nonstop, led me to do just that. I also chose to work from home, and of course, that allowed me to be a serious yard-birder when I was too busy with work to go traveling for birds.

While I was in law school, Dave had also gone back to school to change careers to become a church pastor. After I began my legal career as a patent attorney, he began his church pastor career. By 2000, after I had been an attorney for 15 years, he decided that if he was ever going to change pastor jobs he needed to do so before he was too old to get a new job. My input was requested on where I'd like to move, and I mostly nominated south-western places where new birds awaited me.

The church in Fort Worth came through with the first job offer for him, and we jumped at it. There were great people on the search committee, and just as importantly for me, great birding possibilities in Texas. It didn't hurt that the Texas State Bar was not going to require me to take another exam to practice law there. The house and yard that we bought were in an older 60s subdivision, with one large pecan tree and crepe myrtles and miscellaneous saplings and small trees along the back yard's wooden fence. Not only was the house picked for its bird-friendly backyard, but also for its having a bedroom convertible into a law office with a window into the back yard, and an adjacent back-of-the-house living room with picture windows all along the wall. It was our first house with a respectable view from inside the house. I added a vast assortment of trees and hummingbird plants to the yard.

A Rhyming Summarized Part of My Personal History – 1968 to 2009 (4/12/09)

So, we decided to head up north in our van,
Almost 41 years ago.
Two thousand miles on the bumpy Alcan,
Mostly winding, and very slow.

Then we decided to return to school-Madison,
The liberal place of our past.
Once educated, we were no fools,
We decided to go to Oregon, fast!

Of course, we decided after five years of rain,
Somewhere with more variation was preferred,
And so, it was plain, it was time to go east
To a land less wet and less absurd.

We stayed in NC a very long time,
In fact, it looked like there we would die,
But instead, we decided on a southwestern clime,
And said a very tearful goodbye.

So, have we decided to stay in Fort Worth?
It's anyone's guess; of that, we are sure.
To the day of one's death, from the day of one's birth,
Who knows if it's home or another detour.

During our 10-year Texas stay, I went from being a person who periodically goes on trips to see birds to a person who is a fanatic birder. More below. After the ten years in Texas, my husband decided to retire from being a pastor and to return officially to meteorology. He'd never really left the field, with his main non-working activity being programming his computers to do great and wonderful things with weather data (interspersed sometimes with very unpastorlike words erupting when there was a glitch in the programming process, the data sources, or the weather itself). The last year before he began seriously applying for a position in the weather field, he volunteered one day a week at the Fort Worth Weather Service office so he could get up to date on the technological developments and changes in office procedures that had occurred in the more than 40 years since he'd last worked for the federal government.

Again, as he began to submit job applications, I hopefully guided our choice of potential new locations mostly to areas that might have new and different birds. The result was our next location, Rapid City, South Dakota, where he obtained an entry-level intern position (due to his long hiatus from the meteorology field), and where a spectacular array of birds awaited me. Again, we sought a house with a nice yard, a room with a view on to the yard, and a place where I could put my home office. Because our budget did not allow us to buy a house that was in good shape and that also had a good yard, we went with the best house that we could find and afford and set out to improve the prairie yard by planting bird-attracting plants for hummingbirds and berry-loving birds, as well as to provide perches and shelter.

At that time, I had no idea if we would remain in South Dakota, or if we would eventually move somewhere else. While we loved Rapid City and our return to the temperate (not "subtropical") lands of my youth, I knew that it might be that to be employed as a real forecaster (his goal) and not as an intern, he might eventually need to apply elsewhere. As had always been the case before, when it came time to decide on where I was going to "allow" him to apply, I voted for it being a bird-worthy place. When a forecaster position in Anchorage was advertised, he applied, and we were delighted when he was offered the job. While I had sometimes gone birding during our 1-plus year stint in Anchorage as newlyweds, I had not been a fanatic birder then and would never have considered doing an Alaska big year, if I had known what a big year was. This time was different, and I dove into birding there with passion (see below).

Once Dave and I had received our PhDs and moved away from Wisconsin in 1974, I had assumed that we would never move back. Imagine my surprise on a day in 2020, when he and I sat down in our Anchorage house to discuss when we might retire and where we might live after that, when he (the native Ohioan and not originally from Wisconsin) suggested that we might consider moving back to Madison, where we had met. While my usual request when discussing moving to a new location had been that it needed to be someplace new and interesting to bird, I realized that we had already lived in so many diverse geographic locations that I could consider moving back to Wisconsin, even though there would not be likely be new birds there.

Because it was the middle of the Covid pandemic and because we were way up in Alaska, we did all our house-hunting online. It soon became apparent that nearly everybody else was also looking to buy a house, and most of them also seemed to want to live in Madison. Although prices there seemed to be high, most of the places that appeared to fit our requirements were immediately snapped up. When we broadened our search geographically but kept it in Wisconsin, we got closer to being able to make a bid on a house before someone else bought it. Eventually, to my surprise and thanks to Dave's finding it, not only did it turn out that our new home would be in Wisconsin, but also that we were going to move back to Wausau, where I was born. With only online viewings of our possible new house, we purchased it and embarked in May 2021 on the nearly 4000-mile drive back to Wisconsin through a pandemic-panicked Canada, which did not want people driving through it. A long story. And so, that is where we now live.

Childhood Writing

Excerpts from my early notes on birds, written when I was 9 or 10:

April 28: saw a nest. Thought it was a meadowlark nest...

April 30: saw the meadowlark fly from the nest. Went over there after a while and saw 3 eggs, one small one brown with white spots and two larger ones a bluish gray with brown spots on it. Each of the large eggs had a hole pecked in it.

May 1: found another meadowlark nest with same amount and color of eggs. The big ones were again cracked.

May 3: went out to the field to see the second nest. No eggs were there.

May 4: no bird was sitting on first nest. The eggs were cold.

May 17 (my birthday): Got a bird book...

[miscellaneous tales followed of ducks brought home by Daddy, many other nests found such as Chipping Sparrow, Catbird...]

June 29: A baby robin was out in the garden. I held him and almost kept him, but the mother robin made too much fuss.

July 1: the shrikes are back...

Following are poems written when I was in grade school (as is obvious, I think). As mentioned again below, the prompts or "inspiration" such as it is for each of these was Wisconsin Public Radio's "Let's Write" that some of our grade schools teachers tuned into once a week. I do not specifically remember writing any of them, but they were carefully printed by me in a notebook that I kept. Unlike my later writing, most of my earlier writing is not about birds. I usually illustrated each poem with colored pencil drawings.

My Experience (unknown time, unknown prompt, but possibly on the US space program)

One day when all was quiet on Mars,
I looked up and saw something coming through the stars.
It was red, it was glowing, it was shiny and bright.
I felt my head—was I seeing things right?
Closer, closer, closer it came,
And then on the side, I read a name.
Pop, bang missile No. 6.
Boy was I ever in a fix.
Then all at once a meteorite
Flashed into the scene, shining bright.
It struck the missile on the side.
Pop, bang missile No. 6 had died.
"Yippee!" I cried.

Pet Shop (unknown time, probably a prompt on what we wanted to be when we grew up)

I want to work in a pet shop. I want to water all the pets.
I want to walk over where the birds are, where a greenish parrot sets.

He preens his pretty feathers, and then in a saucy way,
He says, "Hello, how are you? Give me a cracker! Hey!"

A monkey's in another cage. He'll like the cage's bar.
I'll walk over to another cage which isn't very far.

I'll look at the dogs, I'll look at the cats.
I'll look at the mice. I'll look at the rats.

I'll like them all, so I'll stay
To work in the pet shop for many a day.

Autumn Leaves (October 1957, when I was 11)

As I was taking a walk with the brisk October air,
I stopped to look, I stopped to stare.

Leaves were falling, slow and with grace,
Each one falling into its own place.

As I listened intently, I heard in the air,
A whispering sound like someone was there.

"Hurry up, hurry up, it's going to start,"
Someone said and then, "Do you know your part?"

The play began, fast and furious,
I listened closer; I became more curious.

The leaves were putting on a play,
Before they'd sleep the winter away.

When it was finished, I walked home to my place,
A smile written all over my face.

For now, I knew what happened before
The leaves went to sleep on the soft forest floor.

Boss Rooster (unknown time; clearly, I had spent some time watching our chickens' behavior)

The Boss Rooster in every flock watches the hens like you watch a clock.
He will not ever leave them.

He not often deceives them.
When he's running around,
He makes a funny clumping sound.
His feet seem to stretch as far as a man's.
He then puts them down as hard as he can.
To crow in the morning, he's always the first.
His noise is the loudest. His noise is the worst.
When he finds some grain on the ground,
He calls the others all around.
And then when he's done with his food,
He goes into his sleeping mood.
He calls the hens all around,
As if he's found some food on the ground,
But then he goes to sleep,
With the others around him in a heap.
Now that's the way Boss Roosters are –
All of them, everywhar.

Fall (unknown time)

Fall always comes with a rustle of leaves
That go fumbling, tumbling down.
Rust, gold, yellow, orange, and red
Twirling around and around.

Children go to school in fall,
Woodchucks eat and eat.
Pumpkins really become ripe.
Children trick and treat.

Birds begin their southern flight,
Grasses become old and brown.
Fall is a wonderful time of year
With leaves tumbling all around.

The Thermometer (unknown time)

I feel good but it says I'm sick.
Oh, oh, oh what a trick.
I guess I'm sick.

The Haunted House (unknown time)

The haunted house on Tumble-Down Road
Is owned by a frog and rented by a toad.

An ugly old witch with a lion on a chain
Guards the house during sunshine or rain.

Ghosts rattle and clank all through the night
Scaring any human being into a fright.

Now if you are ever advised by a toad
To go into a house on Tumble-Down Road,

Please, please do not ever go.
It is too scary. I've been there. I know.

Winter (unknown time)

Winter is a chilly time, winds blowing through the sky.
Icicles hanging from the roof. Drifts piled way up high.

Some cardinals on the feeding station, some blue jays in the tree,
Some chickadees on the windowsill, looking in at me.

Children sliding, skiing down the hill not far away.
Children skating on the pond, playing winter play.

Winter is made of all those things, all combined in one.
Winter is a chilly time, but then it's lots of fun.

BIRDING TIMES, A LIFE IN RHYMES

My Reward (probably winter, 1957-58)

An oak am I but frightened too.
For do you know what I must go through?
Winter's coming, cold and fast,
And I'm afraid that I won't last.
Oh, here's a squirrel, and look what she's doing.
She's scratching and pulling and biting and chewing.
She's building a nest right on my side.
I'll protect that squirrel, I say with pride.
So, all through the winter I hold her fast,
Coming through bravely from every blast.
And in the spring, she stays in the nest,
And rewards me with her very best.
For three little squirrels and their mother so gay,
Are living in my branches, hooray, hooray,
And all day long they play and play.

Mr. Goldfinch (January 1958)

Mr. Goldfinch, a pert little fellow
With black spots on a ball of yellow,
Has a jaunty black cap pulled over its eyes,
While per-chick-o-ree, per-chick-o-ree he cries.
Dandelions present their golden tops.
Then into the scene Mr. Goldfinch pops,
Toward the dandelion plant he flies
Now I'll tell you I can't believe my eyes
For both he and the dandelion look the same
Which is him I cannot name.
But he then flies away with seeds
To give his nesting wife some feed
That's the little goldfinch, so very pert.
See if you can't find him; it won't hurt.

Chick-A-Dee (probably 1958)

A saucy black cap
His tail a-flap
He's chipper and pert.
Quite a flirt.
His beady eyes
Look toward the skies.
He's a friendly bird.
He comes at my word.
He looks around,
Sees a mitten brown.
He sits on my mitten.
His wings stop flittten'.
A bite he eats,
Wow! What treats!
Another bite,
And he's into flight.
He seems to say,
"Good-bye for today"
And he's off to play.

Note: as discussed below, when we lived at the Mosinee farm, I eventually convinced first the Rock Pigeons that lived in the hayloft high in the barn, and then a couple of Black-capped Chickadees, to hop on to my hand for cracked corn. I can see myself in an old dark green wool coat made by my mother and warm woolen mittens, standing stock still and oh, so cold on a Wisconsin winter day, with my hand outstretched, waiting for birds to land on it. Which they often did, before I gave up and raced back to the house to get warm.

Snowflakes (probably, January 1959)

Snowflakes, snowflakes, snowflakes all around.
Snowflakes, snowflakes, falling softly down.
Snowflakes on the ground, snowflakes in the trees.
Snowflakes on the wind, snowflakes on the breeze.
Snowflakes falling down, having lots of fun.
None of them the same, yet all are made by One.

Home with the Birds (unfinished; to tune of "Home on the Range")
(probably 1960 when I was in my mid-teens)

Oh, give me a ring
Where the birdies do sing
And the warblers warble and play
Where always is heard
A cute little bird
And the sky is filled with them all day.
Chorus: Home, home with the birds
With the meadowlark, warbler and jay…

Outside (unfinished; probably late 60s)

Leaves rustling in the summer breeze,
Wispy fluffs of cloud in a sky-blue sky,
Tiny birds chirp in the far-off trees –
A wonderful world to ear and eye.

Shadows and sun on blades of grass,
Chimney Swifts twitter as over they pass –
There's beauty and greenness and sun all around…

SPECIAL BIRDS AND OTHER CRITTERS, AS I WAS GROWING UP

The following paragraphs were originally begun when I was a child or teen, before I became an adult. Some have been updated for later related observations or happenings. Living out in the country with acres to roam, filled with birds and other animals, my childhood was filled with various wild animals that for one reason or another were captured and turned into what might loosely be called "pets." Stories about some of my most memorable pets follow, as well as stories of particular wild birds that made an impression on my very impressionable self. At that time, I did not consider myself to be a birdwatcher, but rather, my hobby was "animals."

In the Beginning...Brown Thrasher

The first memory that I have of a bird is of a particular Brown Thrasher on our Mosinee farm. A grassy lane extended from behind our barn across the fields toward a distant jack pine woods. When I think back, I'm amazed that our parents allowed us to roam our farm unsupervised, far out of sight of the house. On one memorable day not long after we moved to the farm, I was headed down that lane. I have no idea if I had a goal in mind, or was just exploring, or even if I had ever wandered that way before. All I remember is that a rusty-colored, long-tailed bird dove across the lane ahead of me, about three feet off the ground, and disappeared into a hawthorn/hazelnut(?) bush. I was completely entranced, wondering what had become of it. I pushed the leaves aside to try to find the bird. There in front of me was a bird nest.

Looking back, I realize that I have no proof that what I found was the nest of the disappearing bird, but I've always assumed that it was. That day was the beginning of my love of birds, and of looking for and finding them. It's good that my first bird was a distinctive one – there are no other likely central Wisconsin birds that are rusty-colored and have long tails.

My parents soon understood that I had become very interested in birds and bought *Birds: A Guide to the Most Familiar American Birds* (a Golden Nature Guide, by Zim and Gabrielson). They soon bought two more bird books (Pough's *Audubon Bird Guide* and *Audubon Water Bird Guide*) and a basic pair of inexpensive binoculars. After that I took my much-loved binoculars, a little spiral-bound notebook, a pencil, and the land bird book outside whenever I could, to begin to open the world of birds. I think that my love of bird books was the cause of despair and guilt that I felt a year or so later when I discovered to my horror that I'd left one of them out overnight and that it had been soaked by the rain. There was no question of replacing it – it still could be used. I still have that bird book, with its pinkish, but still usable, dried rain-blurred illustrations, a souvenir from my earliest bird-watching days. And often when it rains, I feel a mild panic that maybe I have once again left a valuable thing outside.

The Song of Meadowlarks

The little spiral-bound notebooks that I kept my bird lists on as a child simply record my meadowlark sightings as "meadowlark" without indication of species. Meadowlarks were common in our fields in the summer, launching up into the air as we passed, singing beautifully from fenceposts and walking purposefully across the lawn. The Golden Guide bird book that I had, which was easier for a beginner to use than Pough's guide, simply showed a meadowlark. Although it mentioned that there was such a thing as a "Western Meadowlark," it did not elaborate on it. I definitely had no clue that not all meadowlarks were the same. Imagine my surprise therefore when one morning I saw and heard a meadowlark that clearly did not know how to sing correctly. Instead of having a glorious bubbly warble, this bird just managed to utter a few clear notes.

Unlike today, when I have recordings of all possible birds, and quite a few impossible ones, in those days I did not have any taped songs (nor did I have a computer nor was there an internet). Eventually I figured out, by reading the birdsong descriptions, that our original Western Meadowlark population had been infiltrated by Eastern Meadowlarks.

Years later, when I went back to visit my parents and wandered around the fields where I'd grown up, I found there seemed to be roughly equal numbers of each species of meadowlark singing in the fields. Unfortunately, most of the fields were no longer there, much of my former haunts having turned into subdivisions.

As I am putting together these memories, I would note that now (in 2024) it is very difficult to find a Western Meadowlark in Marathon County, and there are not very many Eastern Meadowlarks either.

Tweedledee and Tweedledum

One day my sister, my Daddy and I went out to the feed room (where my parents prepared the feed mixture that the mink ate). When we went into the feed room, we heard a rattling noise in the chimney. We wondered what it was, so Daddy took the chimney apart. In it we found a starling. Out it flew. We tried to catch it, but it flew out the door. After it flew out the door, we looked in the chimney for more starlings. We heard the rattling noise again, so we thought there was another starling in the chimney. We shut the door before we looked for the starling. We found one starling and chased him out of the chimney into the feed room. We cornered him. Daddy got a pen, and we put the starling in it. We put a paint can over the hole in the pen. Then we went back to the feed room. We got another starling out of the chimney and put him in the pen with the other starling, and they became our two "pet" starlings.

Rock Pigeons and Chickadees

Rock Pigeons (once called "Rock Doves") were introduced to the US during colonial days and for many years have been abundant across the country. When my parents bought a farm in the country, they unknowingly bought a flock of Rock Pigeons. As a child it was exciting for me to climb up the wooden ladder to the hay mow in the barn. I never knew what I might find as I spooked up the pigeons that roosted and cooed up there. Sometimes I could find an ugly squab, a fat, pin-feathery baby pigeon, on the hay. I was never really tempted to bring one down from the hay mow though – finding it was enough.

What I did do often, however, was to take a handful of cracked corn chicken feed and stand outside near the barn, my hand outstretched, hoping to lure the pigeons in for a meal. Finally, probably in the winter when food was harder to find, pigeons began to come down, landing on my head and hands – a Wisconsin little girl version of St. Francis of Assisi. After that, I could often be found, shivering but happy, feeding the birds.

Even more exciting than pigeon feeding, however, was the first time that a Black-capped Chickadee dared to land on my outstretched fingers, and to grab a piece of corn and flit off. I don't remember how often after that I was graced by a chickadee, but it remains one of my most precious memories.

Ollie

One Saturday morning when Mama was cleaning, she heard a tap on the bedroom window. She told Ann and me, and we went out to investigate. There on the ground lay a little bird and standing over it and pecking it was a robin. I had just been studying the bird book, and I exclaimed, "That bird is an Ovenbird!" The tiny bird was breathing and when it recovered enough to move around and start limping away, we caught it. The little Ovenbird had a broken wing. Feeling sorry for it we put it in an old birdcage hoping the wing would mend (please note that this was in the days before the Migratory Bird Act or any other known prohibitions on keeping migratory birds; it is now illegal to capture and keep a bird without a permit).

The Ovenbird's wing did not mend, but the bird, which we named "Ollie" (for its olive color) stayed alive. As with many of our wild "pets" Ollie was fed mink food, which consisted of a wet mix of ground meat (beef, horse, chicken, sometimes seal), ground fish, cereal and vitamins, on which he appeared to thrive. We always moved carefully near Ollie's cage so as not to frighten him, and he seemed to settle in as much as a wild bird could do.

As children will do, we sometimes stuck our fingers into the cage to see what would happen. As time went on, Ollie developed the habit of sidling over on a perch toward us and letting us rub the top of his head. He mostly was a quiet bird, but usually when my mother turned on the vacuum cleaner, he would break into song, stopping suddenly when she turned off the cleaner (his singing is why I assume he was a male).

We kept Ollie for 18 months, 6 days. Later I found that there were Ovenbirds, which are ground-loving w with olive-green backs and a black-bordered orange cap, regularly present in our jack pine-birch woods in summer. We often heard their distinctive two-note call that others have said sounds like "tea-cher, tea-cher...". Even now, every time I hear or see an Ovenbird, I immediately remember Ollie, and it brings back my childhood.

Other Childhood Warblers

Warblers are probably the main reason I stayed a birdwatcher and became an even more serious bird fanatic. The joy of standing quietly in a springtime woodland with unknown birdsongs raining down on my head and fascinating glimpses of all the colors of the rainbow flitting from branch to branch on my birthday in mid-May is one of my most moving, joyous memories of being a child. It didn't take me long to learn that you saw much more if you stood absolutely still. Even rabbits ignored me, one of which once nibbled on my shoe. It took me a lot of work to identify even a small portion of what I saw, but the satisfaction at doing so was great, and still is!

Chicken-type Birds When I Was Little

As a beginning birder, and even now in my mind, I grouped the grouse, quail, pheasants, prairie-chickens and sage-grouse all together as "chickens". Our Mosinee farm had four different wild chickens.

Ring-necked Pheasants had been released for hunting in the area but were not often seen. The major exception was "Ringie," a pheasant that somehow became "catchable" which I believe was due to his flying into one of our farm buildings. Whatever the reason, Ringie, a gorgeous adult male pheasant, left his probably brief life in the wild and joined our menagerie, having his huge run in the barn next to but not among the chickens, for years as I recall. My memory does not include how or when he left our family.

The other wild chickens on my parent's land were always wild. We heard Northern Bobwhites often, whistling across the fields, and sometimes saw them darting across openings. My clearest memory of one was the one my father, with his perfectly matching whistling, lured to within 15 feet of us as the bobwhite tried to find the hidden intruder in its territory.

Early on another spring morning when I was heading out to see what birds I could see, I heard the distant sound of a tractor starting and then putt-putt-putting to silence, over and over again. I felt myself commiserating with the poor farmer, until suddenly I realized that it could not be a farmer. A farmer would have given up long ago. I'm not quite sure what triggered the light bulb in my head, but all at once I realized that I was hearing a drumming Ruffed Grouse! With diligent quiet searching I found the drummer on a low slanted log, telling the world that it was spring, and he was ready and eager for it. For quite a few years after that, I heard Ruffed Grouse in our birch-pine woods or behind our land near the creek. I didn't always seek them out, but I've always treasured the times that I saw one drumming or flushed one up as I walked through the woods.

A one-time delight due to wild chickens on our land was the spring when Greater Prairie-Chickens, undoubtedly wanderers from south of us where they were known to breed, came to a flat spot in an old cornfield on our land, and we got to hear and watch their breeding display. There probably are not too many people who have had prairie-chickens as yard birds, and they didn't stay long in ours.

Birds of the Half-light and Night – Snipe, Woodcocks and Whip-poor-wills

When I was growing up, on many spring evenings as the sun was disappearing, we could go outside the house on our lawn and hear the distant and sometimes overhead Wilson's Snipe (then called Common Snipe) as they performed their breeding display. Sometimes we could see them high in the sky.

Similarly shaped American Woodcocks lived, and presumably bred, in our woods and in the woods down by the creek behind our house. When I went for my predawn walks in late spring and early summer, I regularly heard the "peenting" sound of displaying woodcocks on the ground and then sometimes witnessed one of them launching upward, usually across the road that ran down to the creek or flying out of the nearby aspen saplings down toward the creek.

All summer long but only in the dark of the night we heard Whip-poor-wills, which sounded like they were calling from our woods. Not being comfortable with walking through the woods in the dark, and not knowing to try to find them perched on a limb or on the ground during the day, I never saw one of them until decades later in Texas during migration.

It's odd how the sound of a snipe or a woodcock or a Whip-poor-will now bring back the somewhat eerie feeling that there was a world out there that I didn't know about and could not see.

The Kingbird Nest

On June 30, 1960, I found a kingbird nest (Eastern Kingbird) in a cherry tree out in our field among some small groups of trees. The nest was about 10 feet up in the cherry tree in a crotch of the tree near the trunk. The parent birds were flying hurriedly back and forth as they found it impossible to fill their three nestlings' mouths.

As I approached the nest a few days later many yells and screams and caws filled the air. I saw about seven kingbirds flying madly about and chattering noisily. Two crows cawed unhappily and flew away being very much pestered. The kingbirds dove down and around and under the crows as if to harm them. After the crows had left, the kingbirds continued their chatter awhile and satisfied that the harm was gone resumed their feeding of the young. They didn't seem to mind me. They probably were used to me.

One day when I went out to see the nest, the kingbirds were feeding the fledglings as usual, but one baby was not in the nest or anywhere around. One was still in the nest, and one was perched precariously on a branch a few feet away, chirping unhappily. The parents must have thought the youngsters were finally old enough to leave the nest because a few days before that I had seen a baby bird hop to the edge of the nest and be firmly pushed back into it.

Corvus

One of my favorite things to do when I went for walks was to look for bird nests. The crow nest that I found when I was 15 years old was one of my easiest finds. Even from outside the small group of jack pine trees, I could hear the raucous cries of baby crows as a parent approached and arrived at the nest up in one of the pine trees. Immediately I decided that I needed a pet crow. Maybe I could even teach it to talk! I have never been a tree-climber, so I lurked under the tree as often as I could get out there, thinking that maybe one of the nestlings would fall out of the nest.

Days passed with the crow babies just getting louder and louder but staying in the nest. Then, one eventful day, one of the apparently newly fledged crows was flapping clumsily on a branch that was almost within reach. I raced over, causing the crow to take off frantically and eventually crash-land under a tree. I am sure I yelped with elation as I lunged forward and grabbed it. I toted my prize home, clipped its wing feathers, christened it "Corvus", the genus of crows, and put it in an empty mink cage.

The summer days that followed were idyllic, as I crawled around in our yard with Corvus perched on my shoulder riding along as I crawled. Whenever I caught an insect, usually a nice juicy grasshopper, I handed it up to Corvus, who gobbled it down. Corvus seemed to transfer easily to being fed by a human instead of a crow. Sadly, Corvus's life ended prematurely when a mink that had escaped from its cage, grabbed Corvus through the wire of Corvus's cage and killed him. I felt terrible that I had caused the death of Corvus by putting him in harm's way, and never tried again to have a crow for a pet.

The Day They Bombed Corvus (written June 24, 1961)

Took Corvus out. Corvus took a bath near a leak in the hose. He stood on the mink pelting stand and dried himself, ate some food and drank water. The birds finally noticed Corvus. An oriole dived at him and scolded him loudly. The female oriole also dived at him once. The male oriole kept at it. A kingbird heard the commotion and arrived, making shrill noises. He bombed once and then without even stopping to perch, he swooped again and again, just barely missing Corvus. Each time the oriole bombed, or the kingbird did, Corvus ducked and cawed as if he were being fed. He then usually hopped a few feet to escape the onslaughts of the angry and courageous birds that were trying to protect their nests and young. A swallow swooped law over Corvus to see what the fuss was about. A tiny chickadee also arrived, but we took Corvus into his pen before we could find out what his intentions were.

The Grackle Episode (probably written 1961, sometime after June 8th)

It all happened when I was walking through the brush near Bull Junior Creek on June eighth in the evening at 8:00. All of a sudden, I saw a large grackle hopping into and out of a small bush and acting quite excited. Something that looked sort of reddish-brown was moving rapidly around under the bush and acting excited. Pepper, the dog I was holding, and I became excited too.

The grackle would hop in the bush and peck vigorously at something, and the reddish thing would make fluttery movements. I first thought it was a thrasher that the grackle was pecking at, and the thrasher was defending itself and maybe a nest. Then I decided that a thrasher wasn't such a helpless bird as that. I then figured out that it was probably a wounded animal that the grackle was flying at.

To make sure what it was I went near. The grackle flew reluctantly away. When I got about four feet from the thing, Pepper went crazy. He literally flew at whatever was in that bush. I went along, not because I was just happening to stroll that way, but because I wanted to save the creature from Pepper's grasp. Even if I hadn't wanted to go that way, I would have. Pepper's leading chain was so tightly in my hand that it, when pulled by Pepper, pulled me and ripped quite a bit of skin off my middle finger.

After getting Pepper away from the bush, I looked in to see the largest live moth I had ever seen. It was a dusky brown and had a large black spot on each of its wings. I wanted to catch it but by the time I had Pepper quieted down, it had sailed gracefully away.

Later, when I got home, I looked it up in the insect book. I found that it was a polyphemus moth. It said in the book that they are about 5.3" wide. The moth I saw was, I have no doubt, almost that big. It was big enough to be mistaken for a thrasher.

The Ground is Covered with Them

That's what I proclaimed excitedly when I saw a flock of Dark-eyed Juncos (then called "Slate-colored") scattered across the center of our circular driveway and spilling on to the lawn near my viewing window in the house. When the rest of my family came over to see what I was jumping up and down about, I expect they were disappointed to see just 20-30 small dark gray and white birds calmly pecking at the ground, birds that we called "air-eaters" because they could eat for hours where there was no apparent food. I do know that the phrase "the ground is covered with them" became my family's phrase for "Lynn is exaggerating yet again".

The Oak Tree

Near our cement block house (out across the fields from our original house on the farm), along an old fence that extended away from the building, was a large oak, probably a red oak. There were a few shrubs and weeds at its base and other smaller trees nearby farther from the house. This tree was a favorite perch for birds for as long as we lived on that property. Each summer, a pair of Eastern Kingbirds (all of which we called "Kingie") commandeered exposed perches in the oak, chattering noisily as they sallied forth for insects and returned to their perches with a flash of their white-tipped tails. I always assumed that they nested there or near there, but their main activity seemed to be showing the world, and any other bird that ventured near, who was in charge of the tree and its surrounding airspace.

Despite the kingbirds, other birds regularly landed in the oak every now and then, including a brave Great Crested Flycatcher venturing from the woods on the other side of the house.

Some summers a pair of Baltimore Orioles managed to sneak in, sing every now and then, and magically produce a nest suspended from a branch. We rarely found the nest until late fall when the leaves finally fell from the oak tree, but we knew there was one before then as we watched the pair of orioles go in and out of the tree feeding their young.

Buzzers (not Buzzards)

When I was in Junior High, or thereabouts, land across the road from us was cleared and sheds were built to house lean, squawky white turkeys that grew into big fat, still loud turkeys before they were taken away. The weeds that grew around the sheds remained uncut, and it became a very birdy habitat. A walk across this field nearly any time of year was sure to flush many little brown birds that I learned to call "LBJs" (little brown jobs).

One summer I was finally able to identify some of them as Clay-colored Sparrows, their characteristic brown face patches and white eyestripe helping me distinguish them from the Chipping Sparrows and other little sparrows. Soon after, I noticed that the buzzing insect sounds that I had foolishly thought to be insects were made by these little birds. Not all songbirds make pretty sounds that sound like songs to us. This knowledge helped me to realize that many of the buzzing sounds in my parents' more heavily vegetated fields were also Clay-colored Sparrows.

Some 40 years later when I lived in Fort Worth, I was delighted to find that the little buzzers as we called them came through Texas each spring, singing as they went. Some springs we had 7-8 buzzers with their soft insistent songs serenading us in our yard for a week or so.

Bird Holding a Long Stick

After we moved out to the farmhouse, one of my favorite bird walks was down to the gravel road that bordered one side of the farm, past the turkey sheds, and then on to land my parents had once owned where there was a meandering creek ("Little Bull Junior Creek").

One afternoon in the early 60's, as I neared our driveway on my return to the house, I saw a bird sitting on the electric line that ran along the road, on the edge of our woods. It was a thin robin-sized bird. The bird did not appear particularly nervous about my approach, so I kept coming closer. Strangely, it seemed to be holding a long stick in its beak, something I'd never seen such a relatively small bird do. As I got nearer, pausing every 20 feet or so to look at it again, it seemed like the stick was hanging off the back end of the bird. Was it stuck there somehow? Suddenly I realized that the "stick" was really a tail! It was a Scissor-tailed Flycatcher, a bird that I had dreamed of seeing someday when I pored over my bird books. In those days (sounds prehistoric) I did not know any other bird lovers nor were there any (as far as I knew) rare-bird alerts where I could report my wonderful sighting.

I learned as I was originally writing this up that there apparently had not been any other earlier reports of a Scissor-tailed Flycatcher in Marathon County, but I understand that there has been one in the last decade sometime. Eventually, if I ever find my notes from this sighting (I always made notes), I can make my early sighting official.
+

Woodpeckers

There were many old woodpecker-attracting trees in the wooded areas where I grew up, and many easily found and heard woodpeckers, my favorite being the Pileated Woodpecker. While I did not write about them as a child, their omnipresence, especially at feeders meant, and still means, that they are important birds to my bird-loving self.

Wisconsin Woodpeckers (8/5/24)

One woodpecker is Hairy.
Another, much smaller, is Downy.
The Pileated is huge,
And actually, appears to be clowny.
The Sapsucker really sucks sap.
The Red-bellied has red on his head;
The Flicker makes loud *wik, wik* calls
The whole head of the Red-headed is red.
All of them climb trunks of trees,
Undulating flight in-between.

All of them easily heard,
And most of them, easily seen.

Thoughts on Being a Birder in a Non-Birding Family

When people I've newly met learn that I'm a fanatic birder and have been since a child, they often assume that my parents were birders and got me started. That is not strictly correct because my parents did not watch birds until after I got excited about birding. But they did make my early birding possible by moving to the Wisconsin countryside, on a warbler flyway, when I was about six years old. Such a move is not a sure way to turn a child into a birder, but it made it within the realm of possibility. Birds were everywhere. My parents did notice and love the world around, the world that included birds, and with their encouragement and in this environment, it would've also been easy to become a lover of deer, or ferns, or flowers, or the earth itself. But I chose, or was chosen by, birds.

I was never discouraged as a child from being a birder, but neither was it on the original agenda of my parents. As they began to realize that it was not just a passing fancy, they bought me binoculars and bird books. And they began to learn at least the common birds with me, and eventually to ask me what birds they were seeing. Without even realizing it, I was becoming more knowledgeable about something than my parents. I was growing up.

My enthusiasm for birds was ultimately caught by my parents, mostly my mother. When I was in college and after I was married, one thing we could always talk about was birds. My mother would regularly report on birds they had seen at their feeders, or when they'd been fishing on a northern Wisconsin lake. When as an adult I began to keep a serious life list of birds that I had seen, I was surprised to find that my mother kept my total next to their phone. When I called to excitedly report on seeing a new bird, she would consult her list and say, well that makes [my previous number plus whatever I had just added] birds that you've seen. To some extent, she, who'd only been outside of Wisconsin for one college year, seemed to share my traveling vicariously. Toward the end of her life, she even shared some of my birding adventures away from their land, driving with me to look for (but not find) Snowy Owls, and to watch Prairie-Chickens and Sandhill Cranes in the fields around their home.

KEEPING BIRD LISTS

Before I ever heard of keeping bird lists, I wrote down the birds that I saw. I had a little grade-school spiral-bound pocket notebook, where I carefully wrote down "robin", "blue jay", "goldfinch", "catbird." I took my pencil and notebook and binoculars with me as I took long walks across our 80 acres of Wisconsin farmland, through small stands of jack pines springing up in little colonies around the mother trees. I usually went down to the creek behind our property on the other 80 acres we had once owned and where we had permission to roam. Paper birches and red oaks and poplars surrounded me. I had no purpose in keeping my day lists except as a record, something I could look back on.

Then in 9th grade biology class, my teacher, Mr. Prohaska, said we were to do a phenology list as spring approached, recording each new budding leaf, each frog song, each flower, each newly arrived bird. It was my first official bird list. I found it to be the most exciting school project I'd ever done. Not only did I glory in the list-keeping, but I also loved making the report to turn in. I illustrated it, and I kept it when it was handed back. And for advanced biology in my senior year, I did another phenology list for the class, with more birds and more illustrations. And I have kept writing down my annual lists of birds every year since then.

In college, the scope of my listing suddenly had to include "state birds." When I was a senior, our plant geography class went to Gulf Shores, Alabama to collect pitcher plants for the university herbarium. The reason I had taken the class was I'd heard that they did an out-of-state field trip each year over spring break. I had not been out of Wisconsin except for a debate trip to Minnesota in high school and wanted to see new birds. One of the other students in the botany class who also was a birdwatcher (I hadn't heard the term "birder" at that point), and I spent much of our days in the swamps scanning the trees and skies, instead of helping gather pitcher plants with the other students.

I realized on this trip that a robin seen in Illinois or Missouri or Alabama could be counted on a new list, a list for each state, just as I'd done annual lists. Suddenly keeping track of things was getting more difficult. Computers had not yet reached the local consumer level, so I embarked on a color-coded 4x6 inch card system – pink cards for Illinois, green for Missouri, etc., and when I ran out of different colored cards, I used different colors of magic markers to color the top edges of cards. That lasted me through college, but our honeymoon move to Alaska, through Canada, brought an additional country and its provinces into my list-keeping. The solution was separate card-boxes for each country, in which the cards were organized by the current bird taxonomic order within each geographic grouping.

But the overall life list concept still evaded me. Finally, to help keep track of things I used a bird book of North American birds to note which birds I'd seen and where and when. This could be updated as I wished. Suddenly, however, all my records were being carried around into the field, and in my car, not always carefully clutched. What if I lost it? The growing records became valuable property to me, irreplaceable. Another bird book was "pressed into service" (as my uncle used to say), so I could have a duplicate list.

During law school, when I first went to work in an office where I was trained to use a computer, the value of the computer to bird recordkeeping was instantly obvious. With some effort I designed a database where I could record the common name, genus, species, family and order, date first seen, countries seen, states seen, provinces seen and other data. The database being searchable, I could use it to create a state or country list of birds I'd seen, but it did not have sufficient detail to give year lists, dates of arrival and departure, bird incidents and observations. That information was still (and is still) recorded in the 4x6 notebook I always took birding. Each year I made a U.S. year list, state-by-state, giving the date first seen in each state.

Then commercial bird programs became available. So, without abandoning my bird book records or my own database, I began entering my bird observations daily into the program, gradually going back in time to enter previous years' records. Unfortunately, the commercial bird program that I chose is no longer available or updated for taxonomic changes, and I no longer use it. Fortunately, however, eBird came along, and I now enter all new records there. I have not, however, gone back to entering previous years' data on eBird, so my records there only go back to August of 2005. I have become compulsive about entering my bird sightings in eBird every day. As of November 27, 2024, I had entered a sighting each day of at least one bird for 2897 consecutive days (about 7.9 years).

RHYMING THROUGH THE YEARS

Rhyming

It is common for a birder to write about birding experiences as I have done before and as I am doing here, but why include poems in the same book? The answer: birding and rhyming have been interspersed and intertwined throughout my entire life. Probably I first recorded in writing my involvement with both activities when I was about seven years old. Similar to bird sightings in my little spiral-bound bird notebook, I wrote down poems. Although my earliest rhymes are undated, they were most likely written then or a little later in grade school, most of them prompted by Wisconsin Public Radio's School of the Air "Let's Write" program (examples above). There were later times when I was involved in activities where we were asked to write a response, and I almost always responded in rhyme, whether or not that was requested. When I have free time or am bored with what I am supposed to be doing, or am in a stressed mood, I often put whatever my thoughts are into rhyme, as will be evident from the rhymes included here.

Although I have written blogs and books and articles about my birding experiences and thoughts, most of my rhymes have not been previously published. Some may think this a good thing, but in any case, in this book more of them are seeing the light of day for the first time. The exceptions to my poems not being previously seen by others are in my first book, *Extreme Birder: One Woman's Big Year*, where some of my big year poems are included, and on the KingBird Tours' web site, where some of the poems that I wrote are given in my unofficial role as KingBird Tours' poet laureate.

As is clear from some of my poems, the need to produce a rhyme bursts forth regularly, whether I intend it or not. I often put my thoughts in rhymes in my head when engaged in other activities. Like birding, it is something that compels me and some days is barely controllable, or just might go out of my control.

When I first wrote rhymes as a child and then as a young adult, I thought (and maybe it was then actually the case) that poems, by definition, rhymed. By the time I realized that rhyming poetry was apparently considered by "real poets" to be lower class, I was addicted to rhyming. Not ever having been one to follow trends in other parts of my life, learning that real poets stayed as far away as possible from rhyming words did nothing to change my habits. Although periodically I have written non-rhyming words that might be considered poetry, I have nearly always aimed to rhyme my poems, if I could figure out a rhyme pattern that said what I wanted to say. But always, in the back of my head is the realization that I am not a real poet; I am a rhymer. I still call what I write "poems," however. Habit dies hard.

The types of my rhymes and their topics are as varied as my life has been. Because I have spent much time trying to analyze why I feel a need to write them, a fair number of my poems are about writing poems. Some of my rhymes that have tried to figure this all out follow.

Rhyming (1/15/96)

Put pen to paper. Something will come.
Probably silly. Possibly dumb.

It may not be polished or fit to be read.
It sometimes comes slowly; often fills me with dread.

Will anything come? Are there words deep inside?
Will something be found? Or has all of it died?

There are days when it's easy, when the words come unbid,
And then there are days when everything's hid.

And then a rhyme comes, or a beautiful thought,
And it's no longer "should" or "have to" or "ought".

It pours out of me; I know not from where.
I rejoice in those moments, no longer despair.

There's a deep need inside to give birth to a song,
To write beautiful poems, paint with lines clear and strong,

To express all the beauty, the sadness, the light,
To set myself free, to give my soul flight.

On the Boat at the Marina (8/31/97)

I said to myself as I journeyed boatward this morning,
"I need to create, produce from within."
And so, I sit here, my pen in my hand,
Not really sure just how to begin.

The words always come if I put them in rhyme,
There's no problem there, and it's really quite fun,
But when I have finished each poetic creation,
I'm not really sure of just what I've done.

What worth is there really in pages of rhymes?
Is there value in singsong, in doggerel, in verse?
Real poets don't do it but abstain from the rhyming.
To them it is silly, prosaic, or worse.

Yet to me it has meaning, while I'm creating.
To say it in rhyme, with the meaning I mean
Doubles the pleasure I find in the writing.
It's clear and precise, tidy, and clean.

Color of Rhymes (9/20/97)

When I feel a poem coming, my inner mind glows.
I see colors and textures not before viewed.
From the day-to-day humdrum of straightforward prose
Bursts a riot of color with glory imbued.

The excitement, the wonder, of being the means
Of converting my thoughts and my visions to words,
Of converting the grays to magentas and greens—
Phooey – no matter how started, it all turns to birds.

Rhyming (4/3/09, I think)

The problem with trying to write a poem to rhyme
Is that the number of words that I need is just wrong for the form that I've chosen.
And when trying to correct that, some of the time
I overcompensate and am frozen.

At a loss on how to change what I've written,
I batter my brain for alternative phrasing,
Which often results in forgetting to rhyme,
And the inevitability of the problem I'm facing:

That not every poem that tries to emerge from within
Is something that deserves to be seen in the light of the day,
And maybe someday when I write, I need to begin
To really say what I mean without forcing it to rhyme.

Rhymes (3/2/21)

It's not in style, to write in rhyme.
They tell me this, time after time,
But what to do when words pour forth?
Flee to the south? Or wander north?
They haven't gone; they're still inside,
Nowhere to go, nowhere to hide.
With pen I sit, and deeply sigh.
To thoughts of flight, I say goodbye.
I'll let them out, these rhyming words-
My yet unseen, created, birds.

Creating Rhymes (~3/9/21)

A thought comes forth, and with it, words,
Words that plead to enter rhymes,
Words that must be said aloud,
Once, or twice, a thousand times.

And still I sit, awhirl with rhymes,
To pin them down is very hard.
Will this word work? No, not at all,
It's difficult to be a bard.

I cannot stop. The words demand
That they must see the light of day.
They must be prodded, poked and shoved
To fit within what I must say.

It must be hard to be a word,
To be a part of what is said,
To bring a thought into the world,
To bring forth life from what was dead.

Let Me Out! (3/10/21)

Two poems are battering their blunt little heads inside my brain as I try to sleep.
Insistent cries and sad little sobs. Should I heed their pleas and set them free?
They do not care if the rhymes be wrong, the meter mixed, the meanings trite.
They just want out, to be made whole, without delay, to see the light.

Writing Poems (8/10/21)

I mostly write poems when I'm filled with concerns,
When something is wrong, when part of me burns.
So, reading my poems will rarely bring smiles,
But writing them did, as I covered the miles.
I don't know what occurs when I put things in words –
It brings me joy, like being near birds.

About My Rhymes (3/16/22)

Got no children, got no heirs. If I did, these would be theirs.
Giving birth to poems might be, done a bit less painfully,
But birthing rhymes just never ends, from predawn past when dusk descends.
From beginning 'til one finally dies, poems, like birds, fill the skies.
Poems erupting, flying, seeping. Poems of joy and poems of weeping.
Good or bad, there is no doubt. It matters not, they will come out.

Rhyming about Rhyming (8/10/22)

Not everyone wants to write in verse. Not everyone needs to rhyme.
Not everyone plays with sounds and words most of the time.
Somehow my writing seems to need the closure rhyming brings.
For me, with rhymes, the earth revolves, and all the planet sings.

More about Rhyming (10/24/22)

I write a poem – it might be a mess,
Yet it expresses what I need to express.
Needing to rhyme, yet it must be precise,
Making my point, while being concise.

Rhyme-o-mania, Rhyme-o-phobia (11/12/22)

Rhyming words bounce 'round my head.
I'm not even out of bed!
I can't begin to understand.
The whole thing's getting out of hand.
I try to stop them. I take a shower,

But now the words have much more power.
It doesn't matter what I do,
Those roiling rhymes keep coming through.
I try to quell them. They just keep coming.
Now my mind with rhymes is humming.
I try to make my mind a blank,
But then I see them, breaking rank,
Tumbling, jumbling, somersaulting,
Each one over others vaulting.
Hurry, worry, flurry, scurry,
Thought is naught. All is blurry.
A place unconscious, so it seems,
Is where they come from, just like dreams.
At last, it stops. My mind is clear.
Maybe there's not a lot to fear.
Maybe life will still go on.
When all the rhymes have come and gone.

Rhyme (6/24/23)

There're quite a few words that will rhyme with "bird" –
Word, absurd, blurred and deterred,
Slurred, abjured and also deferred,
Perturbed, stirred and maybe obscured,
Possibly cured, furred, gird and heard,
And maybe lurid, and certainly nerd.

RHYMES WRITTEN OVER ALMOST 21 YEARS IN NORTH CAROLINA (1979-2000)

Birding Thoughts While in Church (12/25/95)

Birding, they say, is my life.
I'm not sure why that should be so.
Yet midst all the turmoil and strife,
It is birding I feel I must go.

Sometimes I think that I'm crazy,
For letting a hobby control,
But at least I know I'm not lazy,
When I make a birding patrol.

At least I'm not hurting people,
That's what my Mom likes to say,
But perhaps I should stay in the steeple
(that's the church) to kneel and to pray,

There are other things I should be doing,
But they're nothing, compared to "to bird",
So, I sit here, once again stewing,
Hoping to hear my God's word.

Birding Obsession (3/16/96)

Back to birding, my obsession.
Is it progress, or is it regression?

What's the reason birds rule o'er me?
What's the future? What's before me?

Will I always seek their presence?
Warblers, owls, bluebirds, pheasants?

Or will I someday be more normal,
Take up golf, or something formal?

Be a groupie, not a loner,
Stop rejoicing, be a moaner?

You could say birding is a duty:
Birds are needed for their beauty.

I strive to keep my soul together
Seeking birds of every feather.

Birds can lift me from my sadness,
Overwhelm with hills of gladness,

Plug the dams of sorrowful weeping,
Burst the dawn from night of sleeping,

Make me know that life's worth living,
Help me do some self-forgiving.

Birds bring brightness when it's gloomy,
Make the world feel warm and womby.

Nothing's lacking: birds are singing,
Feathered treasures, lightly winging.

Loving Birding/Ending a Bird Trip (6/14/96)

Birding, I love it. Let me list the ways:
I love evening owling; I love early days.

I love birding solo at the pace that feels best.
I love going birding with others obsessed.

I love watching birds as they fly, as they sing.
I love how they hop, how they run, how they cling.

I love birds I've seen over ten times before,
That inhabit my world, just outside my door.

I love going places to see different birds.
I love hearing birdsongs, better than words.

I love the delight of the total surprise,
That comes when a bird first appears to my eyes.

I love seeing rare birds that someone called in.
I love seeing round birds and birds sleek and thin.

I love to go birding when it's balmy and nice,
But birding in storms adds excitement and spice.

I love birds in mountains, on lakes and in trees.
I love birds in meadows, in marshes and seas.

When I think really hard about my birding loves:
They even include sparrows and vultures and doves.

There's little about birding to hate or deplore,
Instead of tiring, I want more and more.

I'm sure of all bird things that I can recall,
Ending a bird trip is the worst thing of all.

Trying to Write a Poem about a Familiar Bird (6/16/96)

The Mallard's a bird familiar to all.
It's common on lakes, on roads, at the mall.

Ungainly on land, with a back-and-forth gait,
It crosses the road as we sit there and wait.

The female Mallard when tending her nest,
Is wary and nervous and not at her best.

Compounding her problems is the green-headed drake,
Pursuing her always, on river and lake.

The newly hatched ducklings, all yellow and brown
Are cuddly and cute in their soft fluffy down.

They swarm 'round their mother like...
(I just did not have any enthusiasm for this self-imposed poetic endeavor, and this is where it ended)

BIRDING TIMES, A LIFE IN RHYMES

Wonder (5/3/97)

I wonder as I'm birding. I wonder and I stew,
Why birding's such a pleasure, but only for a few.

What makes it so wondrous, so filled with delight -
The birds that I'm seeing, the birds out of sight?

In Manteo (NC) at the End of a Work Week and before a Bird Trip (8/15/97)

I don't think I can write, not if I write prose,
So, I'll try for a poem and see how it goes.

A sort of slow week, as I looked for replies,
But not much arrived – no big surprise.

I did little chores, a brochure at long last,
And slowly, but surely, the time wandered past.

A bit of excitement as Friday drew near,
Awaiting a call from a client with fear,

But when the call came, 'twas straightforward stuff,
To allow billing hours, without being rough.

With things neatly done, and no more to do,
I packed to go birding, and then the time flew.

Tomorrow, Pea Island, sandpipers and such,
My own private birding that I love so much.

Up early, drive south, see waves, sand and birds,
A day filled with seeing and very few words.

Peace will flow o'er me, my soul will fly free,
Surrounded, becalmed, by the earth, wind and sea.

Fall Is Coming (9/3/97)

September is here. A cold front is coming.
The promise of birds gives joy to my heart.
The stillness of summer with life hot and turgid
Is slowly unraveling, falling apart.

Carolina Bird Club Meeting (10/3/97)

A CBC meeting at Fort Caswell, NC,
My debut on the board, a big day for me.

Exhausted I am. I got up at four,
Birded Fort Fisher and wanted much more.

In charge of the social, a natural fit,
Been moving all day, so it's now nice to sit.

Bald Head Island tomorrow, warblers and peeps*,
Thinking about birding – my heart always leaps.

*Some of the little brown shorebirds are known rather affectionately as "peeps"

North Carolina Birding (12/1/97)

I moved to North Carolina nearly 20 years ago,
And was struck with great dismay at the mosquitos, ticks and heat.
As I finally ventured forth to see the birds that could be found,
I realized, with joy, that the birding can't be beat.

In the winter when the northland is locked in icy cold,
And birds are few and far between and travelling is slow,
The NC coast is full of birds escaping from the north,
And birding's an adventure for those who're in the know.

BIRDING TIMES, A LIFE IN RHYMES

For example, at Pea Island, there are hundreds of Snow Geese,
And Tundra Swans are everywhere a little pond is found.
There are Buffleheads, and Shovelers, Canvasbacks and coots,
And at the edges of the ponds, Yellow-rumps abound.

Late summer, fall, along the coast
Bring unending shorebird skeins,
Peeps and plovers everywhere,
Egrets, sometimes cranes.

Of course, ocean birding is difficult to top.
Many birders come here just to fill their petrel list.
Shearwaters and gannets, boobies, tropicbirds.
Pelagic adventuring that should not be missed.

Some interesting birds are found in forests near the coast,
Red-cockaded Woodpeckers, Mississippi Kites,
Sparrows (Bachman's, Henlow's), Swainson's Warblers too –
Oft-sought birds that can be found in their specific sites.

Although winter birding in the mountains can be sparse,
In spring the mountains ring with melodious warbler song.
It seems that every warbler that's heading northward then
Travels through our mountains singing all day long.

Some of them do linger, and find a place to nest,
Singing into summer as heat ascends the hills,
And there are grouse, flycatchers, owls and other birds whose calls
Are heard in mountain woodlands and over rocks and rills.

The Piedmont, in-between, is a mixture of the two,
Generally fewer birds, but some of them are great.
Birds of open fields, of rivers, and of towns,
In the winter, add on ducks and other birds from 'round the state.

In the heat of summer when nothing seems to move,
The birds are there, but quiet, raising this year's brood.
There are times you can hear them sing,
Or see them gathering insect food.

It seems there is no end to the birds that might come here.
One only needs to get outside to listen and to look
And check the RBAs* and follow up their leads,
Equipped with scope, binoculars, and a chosen birding book.

*RBA: Rare Bird Alert

On Christmas Day (tune: "I Heard the Bells on Christmas Day") (12/25/97)

I saw an oriole on Christmas Day,
I did not know what I should say,
I sang a song of joy instead,
For all the days that lie ahead.

At Merchant's Mill Pond (NC) (4/10/98)

Wandering amidst the trees.
Warblers sing. A little breeze
Stirs the leaves, and far away
A wild goose calls across the bay.
Parulas ratchet high, unseen,
Among the brand-new leaves of green.
A hollow drumming now and then,
A nervous scolding flitting wren.
A distant crow, an Ovenbird,
Seldom seen, often heard.
I'm all alone and peaceful here,
A Goldfinch twitter all I hear.
An annual trek, a wondrous place,
A world of life, of hope, of grace.

Want to Bird (1/18/99)

I just want to bird; if I can't, let me go.
Life must be happening. Without birding it's slow.

I really can't sit, all inactive and quiet,
Like facing a world filled with food – on a diet.

There's too much to do and too little time.
The more time that's wasted, the greater the crime.

The time that I'm held in a seat on a plane
Seems oddly okay; it's hard to explain –

I guess as a means to an end, it's all right.
I couldn't bird now, as day turns to night.

Rhymes Written in and Around Texas (Not Big Year Poems) (2001-2010)

Since discovering birds in Wisconsin as a child I have watched birds in whatever place that I've lived, usually taking care to record my sightings. After we had incomes that allowed it, I began travelling to foreign lands to see new and different birds in new and different parts of the world. About the time this bird-travelling habit was becoming a bit too expensive to pursue, we moved to Texas, and I discovered that Texas was big enough to be its own country. I began exploring the myriad bird habitats in Texas from the Lower Rio Grande Valley in the south to the northern Panhandle, the eastern coast and pineywoods, and the western mountains.

Except for my Texas big years in 2003 and 2005, and my North American (US and Canada) ABA big year in 2008, while we were in Texas I spent most of my time at home, doing legal work, watching our yard for birds, and wandering around the state. It was in Texas that I really learned to appreciate birds because I saw such diversity. Because I was usually inside seeing the birds, the birds often came very close and gave me better views than one can often get when out birding in nature. Yard-birding became a welcome respite from the frantic bird chases in a big year, and from the hassles of going someplace by car or plane or boat to find birds. I could get the birds come to me (or my yard) by what I did to and in the yard. Of course, when the mood struck and there was time, I also wrote poetry while in Texas.

Birder Code (probably written in the early 2000s)

The American Birding Association and other bird groups have codes of behavior for birders to try to limit the damage that they can cause to the environment.

B is for birds and birders who chase them
I is for idiots, perhaps we could erase them.
R is for rarities which make it much worse.
D is for damage that we cannot reverse.
E is for environment; we all want to enjoy it.
R is for restraint; we all need to employ it.
C is for code that's meant to guide our ways.
O is for obedience, for all our birding days.
D is for despair I feel when rules are not obeyed.
E is for everyone for whom the rules are made.

Joy in Birds (early in 2001)

I sit and listen to a philosopher birder.
He's lost me in a swirl of words.
It's too abstract, though embedded there
Is evidence of joy in birds.

The Moorhen (tune: "That's Amore") (unknown time; probably 2002; thanks to CB for the idea)

See – the squat blackish bird,
Looking slightly absurd
It's a Moorhen*.
With his bright scarlet beak
And his cute yellow feet

BIRDING TIMES, A LIFE IN RHYMES

Strolling by.
As he floats on the pond, or the river beyond, I adore him.
He's a sweet little thing, it's too bad he can't sing, my Moorhen.

*The Moorhen is now called Common Gallinule

Birding in the Rain (Unknown date -possibly late 2003 or shortly thereafter)

Just a-birding in the rain, just a bird to find,
Certainly, it's clear, I'm out of my mind.

Everywhere I go, everything is wet,
Still, I look for birds, on this my heart is set.

People are all indoors; no one's out like me,
Not a bird is flying; nothing do I see.

I must be insane, obsessed beyond a doubt.
If "they" catch me now, I never will get out.

Birding through the Years (probably written in early 2004)

When I was a child, I birded as one,
Took walks in the woods in the soft springtime sun.

I delighted in birds, their color, their flight.
How each day their song turned the darkness to light.

The birds were a lens through which my world view
Was bountifully blessed and made ever new.

As the years have gone by, I sometimes have found
That the lens has been clouded or been turned around.

I still sought the birds, and they were still there
[not completed]

Upon Being Asked – How Do You Like Texas Birding? (6/22/05)

Do you fancy a mountain of junipers, pines,
Or maybe a forest with thick hanging vines?

Perhaps you like yucca stretching for miles,
Or is it the beach that brings on your smiles?

You might like the plains that stretch to the sky,
Or the canyons with beauty no one can deny,

Or maybe you really like rivers that flow,
Or deserts, or big lakes, or marshes, or snow.

All of these places are in Texas somewhere,
And in each of the places are birds that are there,

The diversity – astounding; the landscape, so vast
The birding – stupendous. I'm glad that you asked.

Ode to Sabine Woods (a wonderful birding property owned by the Texas Ornithological Society) (8/24/05)

Be there before dawn, with your bug-spray on,
Preferably buddied, bird book well studied,
Your pants tucked in socks, your eyes seeking flocks.
Birds will be coming, hummingbirds humming.
No need to wait, whatever the date.
Though it seems absurd, get out there and bird.
So, it's off to Sabine, the best place I've seen
For building the list or finding the missed
Birds from last Spring, or some rarer thing.

Anahuac (Anahuac National Wildlife Refuge in Texas) (8/24/05)

Anahuac, it takes me back
To gallinules and limpid pools,
To furtive rails and 'gator tails.
Slimy things and fulvous wings.

Just past Winnie. It's filled with skinny
Leaves of green and things unseen.
Keep open eyes. Expect surprise
And great delight in each new sight.

Where Have They Gone (tune: "Where Have All the Flowers Gone?) (11/5/05) By November in my 2005 Texas big year, I had not yet seen the three scoter species that migrate through Texas.

Where have all the scoters gone?
It's November now.
Where have all the scoters gone?
They should be here.
Where have all the scoters gone?
A lake or coast somewhere that's near.
When will I ever learn? When will I ever learn?
I'll check them all again.

Skeeters Am a Hummin' (5/1/06) Mosquitos in many parts of the world, and certainly in east Texas, are a serious concern of birders.

Eau de Deet; oh, ain't it sweet.
You'd think the skeeters would disperse,
But here they come, I hear their hum,
Yet all in all, it could be worse.

I could be tied to work inside.
I could be doing boring things,
But here I sit – this is IT!
I also hear the birdies' wings!

So, I'm a Deeter; bring on that skeeter,
And bring on birds from 'cross the blue.
The birding's swell in skeeter hell.
There's nothing else I'd rather do.

Thanks (5/20/06) This poem appears in the credits in my first book about my ABA big year. The older I get, the more this is likely to be relevant.

I've studied the list of all my birds,
Trying to remember who, by their words,

Helped me put birds on the list,
Yet I am sure I may have missed

Some of you. So please forgive –
My birdbrain's small and like a sieve.

Fort Worth and Points West (5/29/06)

Gray pavement before me, forever, unending,
Deadeningly straight, with only rare bending.

There are trees, there are fields, but they all run together.
There is sun, wispy clouds, but it's such yucky weather.

The temperature, 92. Only vultures are soaring.
I must admit – it's all rather boring.

I'm keeping awake by writing this verse,
So, I guess it really could be much worse.

It could be raining or hailing or snowing.
The wind could be pushing the car with its blowing.

I could be stuck, or at home sick in bed.
I could be lost or imprisoned or dead.

So, this road's not so bad and it's going my direction,
And I've noticed its beauty upon closer inspection.

It's just that the beauty is sparse and dilute,
And obscured by the length of this unending route.

BIRDING TIMES, A LIFE IN RHYMES

Ode to Tony (4/21/07) Tony was our competition group leader in the 2007 Great Texas Birding Classic.

I think that I shall never see,
A leader like our own Tony.
Though he was stuck with women who
Had never seen a Classic through,
He cheerfully whistled and tooted and pished,
In spite of the birds we'd certainly missed.
We listened for owls and other night beings.
We heard lots of sparrows without ever seeing.
We breathed in the sewage and waded through peeps.
We drove through the dark without any sleep.
We gloried in orioles and rallied with rails.
We pored over warblers along countless trails.
But of all of the bird memories I have of the Classic,
The best are the hermit and duck with a mask*!

    *A Masked Duck; also, a note for those who are not birders, you need to know that sewage ponds attract many birds, and therefore, birders must visit sewage ponds to see those birds.

The Classic (4/07)

C is for crazily running around.
L is for listing all birds to be found.
A is for attention we paid to each chip.
S is for stamina to last the whole trip.
S is also for swiftness and speed.
I is for the invisible birds that we need.
C is also for coastal and chasing,
Just to think back upon it gets my heart racing.

Birds (4/8/08)

The meaning of each day is rarely found in words.
The essence of each day is wrapped up in its birds.
Their being and their songs, their beauty and their flight
Turn ordinary days to days of joy and light.

Bird in the Hand (early 2009, I think)

A bird in the hand? I don't understand.
It's a bird in the bush that meets the demand.

Birding (4/13/09)

Some people sit in their houses and stare out the window at birds.
But other fanatics like me, being far too obsessive for words,

Devote a whole year to the chase across the whole country and more,
Trying to see way more birds than have ever been seen before.

The rarities grow on our lists, the adrenaline pumping non-stop.
But do we stop there? Oh no. Our birding is over the top.

There's hardly a difference at all between birding and dangerous addiction.
The thought that birding's benign is clearly an out and out fiction.

Of course, it allows me to have a habit that I hold very dear,
And to avoid the stigma (deserved) that birders are something to fear.

Driving on a Bird Trip (4/28/10)

It doesn't matter which direction I'm headed,
Although as it happens, I'm going north.
My goal this year is: explore Oklahoma.
It's the fifth time I've been, or maybe the fourth.
It hits suddenly, the urge to laugh,
It's a beautiful day, the sky is so blue.
A Scissor-tail flies to a pole as I pass.
I'm going birding. How about you?

After the Tufted Flycatcher (12/6/10)

"Were you chasing that rare bird?"
"Oh dear, I guess you heard…"
"Coincidentally I just happened by,

In time to see it preen and fly.
I wouldn't chase, not anymore.
That's what my big years were for"
"Okay, 'twas really not a chase –
Or maybe that's egg on your face."

Making a Yard for Birds (unknown date in 2011)

You give them some water, it's really not hard.
Throw in some food – they'll take over the yard.
Plant a few trees to give it some style,
Then mess it all up with an ugly brush pile.
They'll drop from the skies to land on a twig,
Some of them small and others quite big.
Quick bursts of color, flashes of light,
Some quiet and shy, some bold or in flight
Surprises will come – take time to look out.
You'll be glad that you did it. Of that I've no doubt!

RHYMES ABOUT ALASKA BIRDING (2000 AND 2014-2022)

Attu, AK (May 2000 - an Alaska adventure, right after moving to Texas) We had other poets on this trip to Alaska. The second poem below was written by Linda Ferraresso, one of my roommates and one of us who were part of the self-named "Murrelettes." She may have contributed to the first one as well. I just can't remember; after all, it was over 24 years ago.

Our trip begins, as full of grins,
We see a tiny saw-whet owl,
We board the plane, prepared for rain,
And we're off to Attu, fair or foul.

As Murrelet Manor unfurls its banner,
The center of our lives for now,
We bike the runways in startling sunrays
And get the birds the winds allow.

Another bird somebody's heard;
We're off to get another thrill.
We all go nuts, as on our butts,
We negotiate another hill.

The pipit patrol, out of control,
Has scoured the grasses and scanned the beach.
The curlew passes through our glasses,
The other shorebirds out of reach.

The food is hearty for our party,
But every calory's quickly burned.
As this new thrush, with a sudden rush,
Deserts us when our backs are turned.

Our legs are tired, near expired,
As daily through the mud we slog.
We comb the hills, the rocks and rills;
We check each pond, each stream, each bog.

As each bird count begins to mount,
We wonder when the storm will come.*
We look for more, with seats so sore;
Our noses run, and brains are numb.

Say "good by" as out we fly,
Though it was not quite as we'd planned,
The trip will end soon, legs will mend soon.
It's been great to bird this land.

*Birders on western Alaskan islands pray for west winds and storms to bring in surprise rarity from Eurasia.

More Attu

Dearest Larry and Attu staff:
Should we cry, or should we laugh?
On the thirteenth it was snowing.
We all got here but our cargo kept going.

Pitter-patter, what's that clatter?
Rattus rattus on the ladder,
Getting fatter in the larder,
But avoiding Walter sure is harder.

Every day we go a-biking;
Otherwise, it's tundra hiking.
Every night we yearn to turn in,
After all day sloggin' birding.

We have wagtails, we have pipits.
Should we chase or should we skip it?
Dusky Thrush, Far Eastern Curlew.
Was it one or did we have two?

And the weather – it's been sunny.
Each bird's costing lots of money.
But they tell us, "Stop complaining",
And they say, "There'll be birds when it starts raining."

Dearest Larry and Attu staff,
Our two weeks here have quickly passed.
As we leave here, we will all grieve,
And in the morning, hope for Reeve*.

   *Reeve Airlines.

On Attu (5/14/00)

And so, we sit, cold and wet,
But don't you worry, don't you fret.
The birding spirit will not freeze,
And soon birdsong will fill the breeze.
Hope springs eternal – they will come!
Bring on the cheer; disperse the glum.

St. Paul Island (May 2000) My first trip to St. Paul Island was a short trip taken there after the Attu trip. I went back that fall.

On the Plane (8/22/00)

Growling the stomach, bleary the eyes,
As hour follows hour, to no one's surprise.

The smell of the food, the lull of the plane,
Cocooned in aroma – it's hard to explain.

It's all I can think of – a yearning intense,
And writing this poem, my only defense.

The food, it will come, in the wake of its scent.
Perhaps disappointing, but still – an event!

Leaving St. Paul (8/24/00)

'Twas the day that I left on the Reeve from St. Paul,
Leaving goblins and dreidels and leaders and all.

The allure of a mudflat, where something might be,
The excitement of tattlers on the edge of the sea.

The terns on the road, the gulls in the bay,
The puffins and murres, just an arm's length away.

The cranes on the hill, the Ruffs on the rocks,
The inquisitive face of a small arctic fox.

The leaders – there was Bruce striding way far ahead,
And Derek, the imp, with a puffin-like head.

With Eric, I got photos of pipers and stints,
And Mike, he's the Mesopotamian prince.

The leaders were great, each in his own way,
If I wasn't so shy, there's lots more I could say.

And the food, oh the food, one shouldn't complain,
It was fine for our breakfasts out in the rain.

The trip was well-run by its great leader Sean,
Who put up with us until we were gone.

April - After Moving to Anchorage in 2014 (4/17/16)

Mew Gulls sit in pairs. Cranes are flying high.
I hear a faint bird song, and another faint reply.
River running free. No ice is in sight.
Green leaves budding forth, growing toward the light.
52 degrees. I used to think that cold.
Now it is a chance for new life to unfold.

On a plane to Nome (tune: "Somewhere Over the Rainbow") (8/7/18)

We flew – over a contrail, way up high,
Out in western Alaska, up in the clear blue sky.
Sometimes I wonder why I go, to see the birdies down below, I wonder,
Yet something deep inside of me, is calling that I need to see, in wonder, wonder,
I know there's no rhyme or reason, yet I go,
To find, feel, delight in all that the world can show.

Nome Birds (9/1/18)

The seasons come; the seasons go.
It's so hard to let them go.
I cannot stop the birds from leaving,
I know there is no point in grieving.
Though all seems grim, soon comes the snow,
They will come back, of course, I know.

Returning to AK with a Birding Group in 2022

Fall in Adak, AK (9/24/22)

This was a wonderful, made-for-us trip for some of my Alaskan and former Alaskan women birding friends, put together for us by Wilderness Birding Adventures.

We get up. It is cold. We shiver and dress.
Make our way to the coffee. Try not to obsess.
There are birds, we are sure, out there in the dark.
Could be a Smew. Might be a lark.
We hop in the trucks, eager, alert.
We slosh through the puddles, track through the dirt.
Pectorals here, a Sharp-tailed that flies,
And then, a delicious, wondrous surprise –
A tiny brown sandpiper, a V on its back,
Buffy-orange breast area, thin legs of black.
Our leaders confer, photos are viewed.
The result – Little Stint; our hopes are renewed.
Then many days pass with very few birds.
Not looking good (our thoughts without words).
The plane's on the tarmac; it's been lots of fun.
Let's bird a bit more, though our trip's nearly done.,
"Naumann's Thrush", then says Aaron, "that would be great."
And unbelievably, almost too late,
A thrasher-red tail disappears into a tree.
Then seen again, it is greeted with glee.
Lots of conferring, our hopes running high –
The decision: in the air as homeward we fly.

Postscript: it's a Naumann's, a thrush new to all.
Everyone is elated! (Adak, in the fall).

RHYMES ABOUT WISCONSIN BIRDING AND MORE AFTER RETURNING TO WISCONSIN (MAY 2021 TO THE PRESENT)

The Trip to WI (5/8/21)

We started our trip, not be plane or by ship,
But by driving to Tok in our car.
It was stuffed, it was packed, there was nothing we lacked,
For our journey to Wausau. So far!

Late August in Wisconsin (8/23/21)

Nothing flits; nothing flies.
Summer sits. Aching eyes.

Pewee call – all's not dead!
Summer-fall: just ahead.

Migration (9/20/21)

Shorebirds bracket warblers. Then the ducks descend.
Dabblers by the hundreds—hard to comprehend.

Wisconsin Fall (10/1/21)

Pulsing with color, mile after mile-
The trees are aflame; makes my heart smile.

Maples of orange, maples of red,
Colors behind me, colors ahead.

Light wispy clouds afloat in the blue,
Blackbirds and chickadees passing on through,

Starkly white birches enveloped by pines,
A marvelous palette of stunning designs.

Sumacs of scarlet, fields gold and green,
Trees upon trees, with ponds tucked between,

Tall fields of corn, crows call above,
Blue Jays and cranes – what's not to love?

Fall Ends (10/2/21)

And then they are gone, those scarlets and red,
Gently laid down on their thick leafy beds.

Bird Sounds (10/28/21)

A chirp, a chip,
A lisping tsip,
Fog envelopes each whispered sound.
I sit.
They flit.
A world of quiet all around.

Where Once (11/19/21)

Where once…where once…where once…
My mind wanders off, goes astray.
The things of the past are not here,
They are not the things of today.

There was land, ragged land, full of trees,
Full of fields, so full of life.
Now the houses stretch onward, forever.
It cuts through me, like a knife.

The beauties of nature, receding,
No longer so easy to find.
The land that I love always changing,
A fate to which I'm resigned (or not).

Spring (4/4/22)

Ponds in fields, puddles there.
Geese are landing. Trees are bare.

Blackbirds flitter. Rain is falling.
Skies are gray, yet spring is calling.

Bringing warblers, bringing growing.
More of sunlight, less of snowing.

Soon will be a greening world,
Blooming flowers, life unfurled.

Clouds are lifting, skies are lighter,
Spring's arriving. Life is brighter.

Rhymes Coming (6/22/22)

The rhymes had stopped coming. Where had they gone?
They weren't there at dusk. They weren't there at dawn.

Perhaps it was birding and mad frantic chases,
The driving, the searching in so many places.

All of my moments devoted to birds,
Not a minute was left for playing with words.

The tall, green-leafed trees, their tops out of sight,
The sun-dappled roads, the bright shafts of light.

None of it noticed, except when I heard
A tree-obscured warble of some unseen bird.

And then like a blanket of chlorophyll swirled,
I was wrapped in a glorious, leafy-green world.

Bunny (7/29/22)

It's good to be a bunny, I guess, hopping on the road with a friend.
It's good to be a bunny, although it's certain your life will soon end.

I bet that bunnies don't worry or fret that things might go wrong.
Bunnies all live in the present and know just where they belong.

Me (8/15/22)

I want to talk with the girl that I was.
I want to tell her the wonders she'll see.
I want to assure her that life will be good,
That she need not worry about how life will be.

I'm here, but I'm there, with my arms open wide.
I am flying down trails. I am stopping in awe.
There is so much ahead; there is so much behind.
There are birds yet to see, and thousands I saw.

With meadowlarks singing and chickadees nearby,
I'm feeling the need to remember those days,
To relive the joys of discovering her world,
To tell her: embrace life - in all things, always.

Birding Is Like Chocolate (9/15/22)

Taking a break from Wisconsin birds
To bird in Alaska, just for fun.
Rejoicing in each little bird that I see,
Not in a chase, not on the run.

Birding's a lot like chocolate, I guess.
No matter the form, the time or the place,
They're so satisfying, yet I always want more:
Two things that I love, two things I embrace.

Obviously (10/10/22)

When I tell people that I am going somewhere,
Some of them ask, "What will you do there?"
But the people who know me will know what I'm doing.
They'll know it's birds, it's birds I'll be viewing.

Rhyming on the Road (10/24/22)

Golden branches. Leaves are falling.
In the distance, birds are calling.
I'm lost in wonder, lost in being,
Lost in hearing, lost in seeing.
The joy of looking. The joy of finding.
The joy of traveling roads a-winding.

On the road, seeing birds.
Much too pleasureful for words.
Words, however, are what I've got.
So, without a single deadening thought,
I'll just keep writing what I've got to say
To tell the treasures of this day.

Early Morning at South Rice Lake (11/10/22)

The water is wide, and so, deep inside
I feel my body relax and breathe deep.

The trees slightly sway in the breeze of the day,
And slowly my body enlivens from sleep.

The swans glowing white in today's morning light,
The ducks bobbing gently on the slight rippling lake,
The world that I see is beauteous to me.
I'm glad that I'm fully and finally awake.

There are times that I feel a strong need to kneel,
To touch my face to the land that I love,
To give thanks for the skies and the wild bird that flies,
For the grass at my feet and the pale clouds above.

Wild Goose (2/16/23) A chase for a Ross's Goose.

I'm in the midst of wild goose chases.
As snow the world around me erases.
I know there was a Ross's near Two Rivers,
But now the icy wind 'round me shivers.

Nearly 400 miles, the day's hardly started.
It's clear my sense long ago departed.
It's been the same as day followed day.
I've chased the birds, but they've gone away.

Wrinkles (2/27/23)

More wrinkles, more wrinkles, more wrinkles and more!
What on earth are these wrinkles for?
They silently slither and creep 'cross my face –

Way too many for my creams to erase.

Thankful (Not Able to Sleep) (03/25/23)

I'm grateful to be grateful.
There's so much that I love.
The person whom I married.
The soft blue skies above.

The waking in the darkness,
With quiet all around.
The walks in springtime woodlands
When trees are filled with sound.

The smells of sun-drenched flowers,
The smiles of new-made friends.
The plans, the daily schedules
On which my life depends.

The doubts, beliefs and wonder
That swirl throughout my days.
For all of it, and always,
I sing my heartfelt praise.

Following Naomi (4/28/23)

There's a story in the Bible about a woman name of Ruth
(that was my mother's name; it is the honest truth).
Naomi she would follow. She made a solemn vow.
They only had each other, as both were widows now.
My "Naomi" is my husband, and it's very strange to say,
Our "Naomi" is a map app, that helps us find our way*

   *We talk together as if the Google map app is a real woman, Naomi, who usually is a pretty good guide, but every now and then seems to deliberately take us down the wrong roads.

Good (4/27/23)

I look, see the sun. The clouds – they are parting!
I quiver with joy. My laughter is starting.
Bad things have happened. I'm sure there'll be more.
But down deep inside, where my "Lynn-ness" I store,
I know that good things will arise and will shine,
Leaving the petty, the grieving, behind.

Lynn (4/27/23)

This is my story. I now begin:
There was a child. Her name was Lynn.
Family size – it was four.
Parents, sister, not one more.
Moved to the country when she was five.
There she found the world alive.
She saw a thrasher, found its nest,
And now I guess you know the rest.

Long Ago (4/28/23)

On the morn of my wedding, my mother inquired,
"Are you sure of this course that today you take?"
I blithely replied, "I can always divorce,
If what I am doing is one big mistake."
Fifty-five years later, still married are we,
Generally, usually, most happily.

MJ* at UW (5/5/23)

"So very many eligible men,"
That's what she said, again and again.
She held out the promise, and that's what we found –
A clean, wholesome place, with men all around.
One of these men (Dave was his name)…
No more need be said…

*MJ was one of my best friends, ultimately my roommate during our senior year, and the matchmaker who said that I just had to go with her over to University United Methodist Church.

Waiting (5/6/23)

Is "silent Spring" a real thing?
I cannot hear a warbler sing!
The gentle breeze wafts through the trees,
Even if I whisper "please,"
And so, I fear,
I cannot make the birds appear.

Why (c. 5/15/23) The first line describes what I saw while out birding one day in May.

Why does a rail cross the trail?
Why is anything so?
What we know is so small,
Nothing at all.
We just have to go with the flow.

At the Wausau Bird Club Campout, 4 pm (6/8/23)

I sit at a campsite.
The air is so still.
A Chestnut-sided Warbler
Is doing his trill.

The Red-eyed Vireos
Are constantly singing.
All of them, each of them
Joy to me bringing.

Extending around me
And up to the sky
Are green leaves that lift
If a slight breeze blows by.

It's odd to be sitting,
Not running, not chasing.
Calmness and quiet
The rushing replacing.

I almost feel normal,
Not hyped, not obsessing.
A gentle surrounding;
A forested blessing.

Campout Morning (6/9/23)

So – overnight I heard a Saw-whet!
Clearly the very best bird yet!
But birds weren't too shabby on this morning's hike,
Birds that I love. What's not to like?
Redstarts and Red-eyes and Red-headeds too.
Goldfinches yellow and Indigos blue.
Flycatchers – Great-crested, Pewee and Least.
All served up in an avian feast.
Susan [Haug] has clearly done it again.
I just need to know – where next year and when?

And Early the Next Morning (6/10/23)

Pewees start the chorus at 4,
Two or three or maybe more.
Red-eyed Vireos join the song,
Then Redstarts eagerly sing along.

Sometimes (6/24/23)

Sometimes when I'm birding, and I look at a bird,
I break out in laughter – it's just so absurd.
A small thing in feathers. It's wild and it's free.
Why do I need it to make myself me?

Sometimes when I sit, all around me their song,
I know all is right, and nothing is wrong.

Above me the sky, surrounding me, trees.
The joy that I feel makes me weak in the knees.

When I hear one so clearly, like a Sandhill or Veery,
The sound fills my soul, and my eyes become teary.
Sometimes it's music, sometimes it's words,
But mostly what gladdens my heart is the birds.

Beginning (6/26/23)

The last bird that I hear at the end of the night
Is the first bird that welcomes me into the light.
A robin today brought the morning to me,
A dawn serenade from a silhouette tree.
Tomorrow? A cardinal, or maybe a wren –
A new beginning, all over again.

Limpkin (6/26/23) Limpkins are large brown southern wading birds that are rare in Wisconsin. I just could not find the one that had appeared in 2023 at Horicon Marsh about 130 miles south of Wausau, even though other birders kept reporting it. I kept trying. After my third unsuccessful trip there, I vowed I would not try again, and maybe wouldn't even do another big year, and I wrote this poem. Later, when others still were seeing it, I tried a fourth time and finally succeeded.

The missing Limpkin may be the cure.
I didn't see it. That's for sure.
Maybe my big years are a thing of the past.
Maybe the last one was the last!
Why have I done them? Just because.
Time will tell. It usually does.

Obsessing (7/1/23)

Some people are obsessed with trains,
Others with weather and others with planes.
To me, these obsessions seem rather odd,
But my obsession came straight from God.
It must be so. It's part of me.
When I came into being, it came to be.
Yet I do admit. I understand,
When my obsession gets out of hand,
It probably isn't preordained.
Probably I should have just refrained.
What I did, I am confessing,
Is give in, again, to obsessing.

On Driving Through Rural America *(7/18/23)*

I'd like to tell them, one on one,
That I am right, that they are wrong.
I might as well just flap my arms,
Fly up high, break forth in song.
Each of us, not comprehending,
How the other can be so blind,
Thinking that calm conversation
Could change the other's stubborn mind.
Somehow, we all must find a way
To soften anger, lessen fears…[unfinished]

Whatever (8/7/23)

Some like big birds,
Some like small,
Some like any birds,
Any birds at all.
Some want to hear them,
Others need to see,
Some say "whatever."
Just like me.

Owls of Yore (8/11/23) When I was writing my book about owls, I spent days poring through my bird notebooks, looking for notes mentioning owls.

I've finally found a reason, for all of these notebooks of words,
For all of these zillion notebooks, filled with sightings of birds.
Buried on all of these pages, my findings of owls I've found,
Owls that were calling and nesting, owls in the air, on the ground.
Underlining, bold letters, exclamations, point to the owls that have been.
The thread of my life, of my being. The future, the now, and the then

WSO (Wisconsin Society for Ornithology) (9/11/23)

Stop, look and listen. What do they say -
The people of birds, whom I'm meeting today?
"Advocacy," "Diversity," "Communicating" I hear.
"What should we do for the birds we hold dear?"
Most of us male, most of us white,
The look of our group, a gray, white-haired sight.
Helping birds that we love, we must do, spread the word
To everyone, to all – for each blessed bird!

On Hearing "Hidden Brain" on NPR (9/21/23)

Cognitive dissonance - I've got it in spades,
I tell myself, always, that everything's fine.
Whatever occurs, it's that that should be.
It's the preordained plan; it's the design.

Where I am, always, is where I should be,
All the alternatives – inferior at best.
My Pollyanna self smiles at the world,
And at night, with a sigh, is able to rest.

Seasons (/9/25/23)

They just keep coming, these seasons, four,
Coming faster than before.
Red leaves, snowdrifts, flowers, then hot,
Just as if a devilish plot
Took out minutes, took out days,
Made them go their separate ways,
Left me spinning, wondering how
I sped so fast from then to now.
Sometimes a moment rose up, shining.
In the midst of memories pining,
Helped me feel it, see it, taste it,
Not to mourn and not to waste it.

Spruce Grouse Bird Dreams (9/29/23)

Birding's a lot about waiting for what may never be.
Birding's a lot about hoping for birds that you're anxious to see.
Birding's uncertain, a gamble, but sometimes it turns out just right –
A reward, so worth all the struggle – the bird sitting there, in plain sight.
Wishful thinking, just now, while I'm sitting, for the 99th time, so it seems.
For now, the Spruce Grouse is only a figment of my endless dreams.

Joy Of Birding (10/14/23) I began my talk on the Joy of Birding with this poem at the Wisconsin Society for Ornithology's first "Unconvention" in October of 2023.

Your joy of birding may be chasing birds,
Or may just be to be where they are.
The joy of birding can be done right here,
Or can lead to places away, so far.

The joy of birding can be as different as
I am from you, and as you are from me.
No matter how each of us defines this joy,
It is something we know, or I hope soon will be.

Another (Unsuccessful) Spruce Grouse Hunt (10/26/23)

I sit in the car, in the dark, in the rain.
What I feel is not just my ongoing pain,
But hope and excitement that this time I will see
The elusive Spruce Grouse. On the road? In a tree?
Breathing in, breathing out. I relax and I wait,
Resigned to whatever will be my fate.
If I see it, what then will I next want to find?
What will obsess me, play with my mind?
Whatever the obsession, wherever I go,
A bird I will chase. That much I know.

The Present Between (11/20/23)

Bare naked branches, stark against gray sky.
Five silent swans, slowly flying by.
Cranes out in the stubble. Soon they will depart.
Summer just was here. Winter soon will start.
But winter's not here yet – Snowy Owls I've yet to see.
I pine for what has passed and yearn for what will be.

Geese (12/9/23)

The sound of geese. It makes me cry.
I feel the weight of years gone by.
I close my eyes. My shoulders shake.
I cannot tell what I should take
From unplanned grief, from longing, deep,
From yearning and the need to weep.
I only know the sound of geese
Provides a blessed, surprise release.

The Answer (12/12/23)

They flit, they fly, I don't know why.
And then a cruising hawk speeds by.

Squirrels (12/23/23)

Ain't I good to the world of squirrels?
Cute little guys with your tails in curls.
Not a word of thanks do I hear.
You eat my seeds and disappear.
It's okay, I guess. You need to eat too.
There's plenty of seed for all of you.

White Question (1/24/24)

Would I ever be able to see –
It seems quite unlikely, impossible to me:
A Snowy Owl, in the fog, on the snow?
Inquiring minds would like to know.

My WSO Plea (01/27/24)

Do you love birds,
think they're pretty or cute?
Do you listen with joy
when they sing, call or hoot?
Do you wander the woods
when the birds fill the trees?
Do you walk on the shore
'mid the gulls and the breeze?
If thinking of birds makes you wish for a way
that you could do something to bring forth a day
when birds and their world would be safe,
then I ask,
that you work with us now
on this most worthwhile task.

Winter Yard (2/10/24)

Swirling siskins circle round.
Cawing crows in chorus sound.
Stealthy starlings steal in fast.
Weaving waxwings wander past.
Morning madness in my yard.
Winter wonders. Winter's hard.

Long-Eared Owls (tune: "Both Sides Now") (03/18/24)

I've looked at trees from both sides now.
I see no owls, but still somehow,
The owls are hidden. I recall,
I really don't know owls at all.

Bufflehead (3/30/24)

A "buffle" on his head?
"What a weird bird," I said.

Before the Arizona Nightbird Trip (4/25/24)

I made a mistake – I just glanced at the wall.
There's a mirror there. That is all.
A wrinkled old lady stared back at me.
Her face was aghast, I could plainly see.
That's the face I will carry downstairs.
A face full of years, of memories, and cares.
But behind all those wrinkles is my certain delight
In the birding adventures beginning tonight!

Dogs, Cats and Owls (5/25/24)

They have come with us through the eons, until now.
Two -- in our homes, in our hearts, on our beds.
Owls, though, have stayed in the wild, flying free,
Not in our homes but perched in our heads.
Charismatic creatures, enigmatic, owls.
What are they thinking as we look into their eyes?
Are they good? Are they evil? What's on their mind?
And always, we wonder, do they know? Are they wise?

Three Owls*(6/28/24)

I should write a poem about owls.
I've written a whole book. I can surely do a rhyme.
Think of their roundness, their eyes.
The words should come easy; shouldn't take too much time.
I close my eyes. There's a large one,
High on a branch, fuzzy ears, golden eyes.
Silently we stare at each other,

And then in the distance, the strangest of cries:
It sounds like someone yelling hoarsely,
"Who cooks for you? For you? For you?"
An actual horse seems to answer –
Owl number 3 after owl number 2.

*Owl #1: Great Horned Owl; owl #2: Barred Owl; and owl #3: Eastern Screech-Owl

Colors (7/13/24)

Birds of red, birds of gold,
Birds of beauty I behold.
Birds of orange arrive to feed.*
There is nothing more I need.

*Northern Cardinal, American Goldfinch and Baltimore Oriole.

Guldan Road (7/16/24)

I love being out, on a road, in the breeze.
A creek flowing by. The green leafy trees.

A Song Sparrow singing, a vireo too.
And up on a branch, an Indigo, blue.

Fields of corn, a chattering wren.
A Mourning Dove coos, so sadly and then

Swallows perched in a row and swooping down low.
Birds to enjoy wherever I go.

Horicon Marsh (8/5/24)

There are Black-necked Stilts that are there, and Limpkins at times.
And others whose names don't fit into rhymes.
And cranes, both Sandhills and Whoopers too,
And birds that I hear but haven't a clue.
Blackbirds – yellow-headed and those with red wings.
And deep in the reeds, a Marsh Wren that sings.
Birds on the water, in the grass, in the air,
So, when you go, you needn't despair.
You will see birds, there is no denying.
You will see birds without even trying.

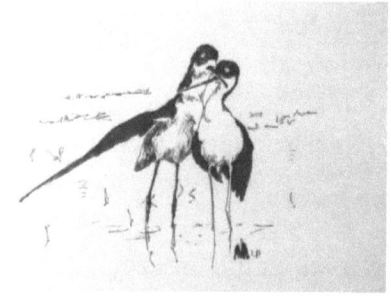

Wisconsin Morning (8/9/24)

5:30 – an owl; ten minutes later, a crow.
It looks like the world, once again, is a go.
A cardinal now sings; the sky is now light.
A hummingbird sips! The world is all right!

Breathe (9/1/24)

Every now and then I have nothing to do.
This only occurs when I shut down my mind.
When I don't let it know what my calendar says,
And don't let it look for what I know it will find.
I look out the window. The trees are still green.
I guess it is summer and hasn't yet become fall.
Where do the days go when I'm scrambling around?
Is life just a maelstrom? Is that really all?
I take a deep breath. I glance at the sky.
I look at the garden and the sun-dappled grass.
I think of the years when I've not stopped to breathe,
And moments like this have not come to pass.
And I breathe again.

LYNN E. BARBER

HARDCORE BIRDING TIMES AND RHYMES

Travels with Lynn

Mostly when I've traveled to go birding, I have not written poems, or anything at all, except birding notes in my birding notebooks. I've been too busy birding or racing from here to there. Sometimes, however, when there were long bus rides or extra spare time, I have been able to write a bit. The first rhyme below is a summary of highlights of some of my earlier trips that did not include rhymes, interspersed with prose accounts of some of my trips taken before 1997, when I began to write more travel-related rhymes.

Summary of Earlier Travels – 1979-1996

An Autobiographical Poem Emphasizing Birding Travels (6/24/24 ff)

I need to write poems about so many places.
Places I've traveled without writing rhymes.
I've nothing but bird lists from so many countries,
So few poem memories of these long-ago times.

My birding adventures (outside of Wisconsin)
Began when I was just past twenty,
With a botany trip to far Alabama.
In the midst of the plants, new birds a-plenty.

As a new bride, a year and more later,
Off to Alaska, we drove o'er "the Road." I'd never dreamed at the time of our dating
Of such far-off travels, to such an abode.

From there, we moved back (for more education) -
A bunch of degrees, and then we moved west
To "Orygun", and rainbows and rain
For five years, we made Corvallis our nest.

A working (and birding) adventure in Chile,
Growing alfalfa and digging in dirt.
Of course, always when I was digging,
For birds up above, I was ever alert.

Our nest wandered eastward in '79.
For over 20 years, Raleigh, our home.
It seemed we were settling, and putting down roots,
But beckoning birds caused me to roam.

A journey to Australia to listen, to speak –
Also occurred in '79,
And of course, I went birding before coming home,
Always a part of my travel design.

Before more bird traveling, we made a few changes.
Went back to school, learning law things and preaching.
Embarked on our new lives, away from a campus.
Away from academia and the days of our teaching.

We also traveled across the "big pond"
To see my sister and watch her be wed,
As well as to wander, explore merry England,
A great place to bird when all's done and said.

1992 - Costa Rica

First, Costa Rica. It seemed to me then,
If only one country I was able to see,
There I would go, bask in the jungles,
Be the birder I knew I could be.

I went to Costa Rica in 1992. It was my first international birding trip and was a wonderful way to start my foreign birding adventures. It was led by Simon Perkins (Massachusetts Audubon Society). The trip lasted 13 days, had 13 participants, and was there on Friday the 13th and the Ides of March. I got over all sorts of superstitions because it was a great trip, and every day gave me new birds and I made new friends.

1993 – VENEZUELA

I was hooked, I found out, so I tried it again
On a ranch near Caracas. It was covered with birds.
The joy of the seeking, the finding, the learning,
Was way beyond my rhyming with words.

My second international birding trip was the next year to a huge private ranch in Venezuela. We stayed at a building on the ranch that at times housed researchers. Every day we loaded up on a truck, sitting on benches in the back. The truck drove to different habitats on the ranch. Because it was apparently the beginning of the dry season, many of the ponds on the ranch were drying up, revealing fish that were gradually losing their wet world. Various herons and other fish-eaters patrolled the pond edges, gorging themselves.

My other main memory from this relaxing bird-filled trip was of a nighttime drive into a wooded area. When the truck stopped our leader (once again Simon Perkins) shone a flashlight upward and there, directly above us, sat a roosting Spectacled Owl, definitely a beautiful spectacle.

1994 – Kenya and the Galapagos Islands

I traveled to Kenya. The birds were amazing.
Hundreds and hundreds I'd not seen before.
Their colors astounding, their names unfamiliar.
It was, I should mention, in '94.

1994 was an unexpectedly big year for my international bird travel – two amazing trips. The first long-planned trip was to Kenya with Sunbird Tours. It lasted for four weeks, the last week being a week-long extension to the coastal area.

The Kenya birding group divided itself into the "mammal van" and the "birder van" so that people in the latter van could try to see, and photograph, if possible, the harder-to-see little birds without making the other people too impatient, and of course then had to spend less time on lions and antelopes. But everyone saw many mammals and birds. My total for the trip was over 700 species of birds, over 600 of which were "lifers," never before seen by me.

One memorable time was on our way in the vans to our huge, fully equipped tents:

We slip and we slide. There's mud all around.
It's rained and it's rained. We feel as if we've drowned.
Now we're stuck in the mud. It's dark, and I'm tired.
I get to my tent. I've nearly expired.
The mud is cleaned off. There's a warrior with spear!
Is this a new friend or someone to fear?
He's my tall, silent guide, from my tent to my meal.
A world far away, surprising, unreal.

I had not planned to go on a second trip in 1994 after the lengthy, expensive Kenya trip, but my husband's purchase for me of a new magazine, *Ecotravler*, changed that. In the back of the magazine was a postcard that could be used to win a trip for two to the Galapagos Islands:

I entered, I won, and we hopped on a plane.
Then to our boat, and our trip 'cross the sea.
Endemic new birds, on the land, in the sky.
A wondrous adventure, for Dave and for me.

1997 - Bhutan (and India)

My trip to Bhutan was in April 1997 with Ben King (KingBird Tours). We flew into western Bhutan, and boarded a private tour bus, which took us across the whole country. We tent-camped at night or stayed in our sleeping bags in various buildings, and then each morning boarded the bus again. Periodically during each day, the bus would stop, and we would all get out to walk the (only) road. The bus would drive ahead and when we reached it, we would climb aboard and repeat. All the in-bus time allowed me plenty of opportunities to write rhymes.

Toward the end of the trip and the eastern end of Bhutan's cross-country road, we happened upon an outdoor community party celebrating the end of the road's construction, where, as visitors to the country we were given seats of honor (old sofas dragged to the area) as an Indian rock group entertained the crowd.

The next day as we entered India, armed Indian military men stopped the bus and entered it, roughly demanding to look at our carry-ons. At gunpoint I was asked to show them my pink soap container, which contained, of course, a bar of soap. Someone explained that they were searching for batteries that rebels could use for explosives. My batteries were in my suitcase, and thankfully they did not bother with those. The trip ended in India without further excitement.

When I showed Ben King the poems I had written during the trip, he added them to a newly created poet laureate page on his website (which as of this writing is still there).

Why, in Bhutan (4/14/97)

I sit in my tent, faint mutterings around.
The birders are resting from efforts profound.

A full day of walking, of searching, of thrills,
Of listening to bird songs and walking down hills.

Why are we here? Why is it fun
To walk in the rain and cook in the sun?

The joy of the quest, uncertain the end
Keeps us all going around the next bend.

The owl calling now makes everything clear.
Because I love birding is why I am here.

Fanatics (4/17/97)

We are in Bhutan, a KingBird Birding tour.
We are all fanatics, seeking more and more.

Do I ever stop and wonder why we are here?
There's no time to do it. That's one thing that is clear.

Ben our leader's gloating; we have found another thrill.
Toes and joints are aching; we have walked another hill.

Something flies above us. Something lurks below.
Lifers I am finding everywhere I go.

Every day is different, yet a pattern I have found:
Waking in the wee hours; walking 'til we're drowned.

Raining, raining, raining. Birding in the rain.
Clearly something's lacking where I ought to have a brain.

Little chirps and twitters, coming from the trees.
Fog is drifting o'er us brought in on a breeze.

Clearly, we are special; there's no one quite like us.
We are heaven on wheels, in our own tour bus.

Now our bus is swerving, to avoid another cow.
Now we're in a snowbank, masquerading as a plow.

Now we're fording rivers, running gauntlets in the flood.
Now we're picking leaches and mopping up the blood.

Other peoples' hell is our idea of fun.
Of course we will not quit – we have just begun!

No more are we strangers – birding buddies now,
Getting all the birdies that time and God allow.

Snoozing after lunching, running to the scope,
Getting way more new ones than we had dared to hope.

Tragopans and trogons, minivets and more,
Babblers, Barbets, buntings, bulbuls by the score.

Dapper drongos, dippers, laughingthrushes too,
Magpies, mynas, minias, robins full of blue.

Partridges and pigeons, fulvettas, forktails, crows.
We get birds with Ben, as everybody knows!

Climbing (tune: "We Are Climbing Jacob's Ladder") (4/19/97)

We are climbing Bhutan's mountains (3x);
Birding Bhutan's hills.

BIRDING TIMES, A LIFE IN RHYMES

Terraced slopes and water falling,
And I hear a strange bird calling,
Oh, it's just all so enthralling.
Birding Bhutan's hills.

Every switchback's higher, higher;
And that bird's a flier, flier;
And the mountains dryer, dryer;
Birding Bhutan's hills.

Now it's getting awful foggy,
And I'm getting very groggy,
And now I hear the barking doggy,
Birding Bhutan's hills.

There is nothing I like better
Than birding while I'm getting wetter
Than a drowning Irish setter,
Birding Bhutan's hills.

There are rocks on every trail,
And cow pancakes without fail,
As we walk o'er hill and dale,
Birding Bhutan's hills.

Finding lifers, finding leaches,
Hearing sighs and hearing screeches,
Learning lessons birding teaches,
Birding Bhutan's hills.

Something's flying to the right.
Can you tell it by its flight?
A bit tricky 'cause it's night.
Birding Bhutan's hills.

What's that song? I'm sure I know it.
If I ID it, I will blow it.
Where's a rock so I can throw it?
Birding Bhutan's hills.

In the tree, out on the end there,
Just above the branch's bend there.
See the head – it seems it's red there.
Birding Bhutan's hills.

Ben has found it; see he's pointing.
My head's bent back, my neck's disjointing.
Oh, it's gone! So disappointing.
Birding Bhutan's hills.

Oh, I've found it, what a blessing.
No more questions, no more guessing [pause to look]
It's no lifer! How depressing!
Birding Bhutan's hills.

In the end my list is longer,
And my legs, they sure are stronger.
I'm a birder. I belong here.
Birding Bhutan's hills.

Bush Chat (tune: "K-K-Katy") (4/19/97) For some reason, I found it impossible to remember the existence of the Gray Bush Chat during the Bhutan trip. I would see a little featureless bird, and ask our leader excitedly what it was, only to learn that it was always the Bush Chat.

B-b-bush-chat; B-b-bush-chat;
It's the only b-b-bird that I can see.
When the b-bus goes over the mountains,
It'll be waiting on each post, each bush, and each tree.

Laughing (tune: "Little Brown Jug") (4/19/97) Numerous species of Laughingthrushes are common in Bhutan but are always almost impossible to locate in the thick underbrush.

"Yo ho ho, they can't see me,
For I am a Laughingthrush"
"Yo ho ho, they'll never know,
There're thousands of us down here below."

Birding in the Rain (tune: "Just Walking in the Rain") (4/23/97)

Just a-birding in the rain. Getting soaking wet.
Torturing my feet and watching minivets.
Just a-birding in the rain. Getting soaking wet.
Wish I'd see the birds and trying not to fret.

People drive by in Druk-trucks. *
They always stare at me,
Shake their heads in wonder,
Saying "who can those fools be?"

Just a-birding in the rain. Getting soaking wet.
Why is it I'm here? Somehow, I just forget.

*big, orange, garishly decorated trucks

Falling Raindrops (tune: old Sunday School song of "Hear the Pennies Dropping") (4/23/97)

Hear the raindrops falling. Listen as they fall.
I am here for birding. I will get them all.
Birding, birding, birding, birding, look at all the birds.
Each bird is a lifer. My joy knows no words!

1998 – ANTARCTICA

I had long wanted to go to Antarctica to see penguins up close and personal. Although by 1998 I was self-employed and no longer drawing in a guaranteed salary, being self-employed meant that I did have time for such a long trip. I again chose a Massachusetts Audubon Society trip for the leader, Simon Perkins, and because the itinerary was shorter than most, which meant that the cost was less. Of course, there were fewer possible birds and there were not the usual South American side trips, but the trip did have a couple of days in southern Argentina after the sea voyage.

The following rhyme tells the story of the birding wonders there, which were followed by a couple of days of storm-tossed terror on the ship.

Antarctica Trip 1998 (2/1/98)

For our Antarctic trip, we boarded the Disko.
Gently it started – the Drake Passage, asleep.
Seabirds soared 'round us, penguins cavorted,
As we steadily steamed over waters so deep.

Perched near the bridge, bins glued to his eyes,
Simon, our leader, exulted in glee.
Each new bird that appeared, so clearly a lifer,
He helped us discover just what it could be.

For hours we stood, midst the circling birds,
As they looped graceful flights that lifted our hearts,
And then just as soon the seas would be empty,
Birds having flown onward to far distant parts.

BIRDING TIMES, A LIFE IN RHYMES

In the rain and the wind, the cold and the snow,
We kept up our vigil, expectant, as one,
Our entire beings absorbed in the quest,
Our life-lifting passion, our joy and our fun.

Blue petrels and prions we learned to distinguish,
Albatrosses - Royal and Wandering, too.
Black-brows were common, willies and giants,
Together they gave us plenty to view.

And then we arrived in deep penguin-land.
They porpoised, on purpose, with grace and in play.
We stood in their midst, a part of their world,
Marveled, took pictures, moved out of their way.

They raced through the water, emerged with a leap,
On shore, or on icebergs, in groups or alone,
Deliberately waddled, and hopped little hops
On ancient worn paths, on ice and on stone.

Looking down at their feet, or ahead to their goal,
Never in haste, both stately and cute,
Their slow steady movements toward colony, home,
Cacophonous greetings, their young in pursuit.

Slowly we began to emerge from our birding,
To gaze at the wonder, the mountains of blues,
Gargantuan icebergs, impossibly drifting,
Unbelievable sizes, incredible hues.

They loomed high above us, surrounded our ship,
Filled our horizons, brightened our days,
Kept us in awe at their beauteous forms,
In sunlight, in clouds, in rain or in haze.

LYNN E. BARBER

And then there were whales, remote and up close,
They held all entranced with their ponderous grace,
Emerging from somewhere and then disappearing,
Increasing the wonder we felt in this place.

As day followed day, full of penguins and bergs,
As we took in the beauty, as it washed o'er our souls,
None of us dreamed of the change that was coming,
That altered our plans, confounded our goals.

As we turned toward the Drake, and our passage toward home,
We experienced a difference in wind and in wave,
Our stomachs and spirits were caught in a vise,
Of towering mountains and shuddering cave.

There was no end in sight to the unending swells,
To the sickening tilting, the sliding, the falls,
The number of sick ones doubled and tripled,
As showers followed storms followed showers and squalls.

A stupor spread o'er those who'd succumbed to the sea,
Patiently waiting in dullness and pain,
Dimly aware that birds, food and life
Continued in spite of the waves and the rain.

And then it was over, the terrible Drake.
We entered the Beagle, returned to upright.
The sun actually shone, the world regained splendor,
The mountains, the skies, our futures, were bright.

There were those on the trip, not birders hard-core,
Who sat and read books, talked, became friends.
Experiences different, yet all were amazed
At the beauty of nature that around us extends.

There's lots more to tell of the birding on land,
Proceeding and following our journey in ice,
Woodpeckers scarlet, and siskins of yellow,
Grebes, coots and ducks and others quite nice.

No doubt, I would do it again if I could,
In spite of the Drake. Because of the birds.
Because of Simon, the others, the views,
An experience too wondrous for limited words.

1999 – FINLAND (6/5-18/99)

This trip was also led by Simon Perkins. One of its main goals was to find northern owls of Europe, which we definitely saw. I guess I was too busy birding to remember to write down when each of the following poems was written during the trip.

Finland

The *Crex** checks, the owl prowl,
Through weather fair and weather foul.
A siskin "sssks", a swift sweeps,
A lark lilts, something cheeps.
A twitting tit, a puffed ruff,
A flushed thrush, some neat stuff.
A rook nook, a crane refrain,
Birding pleasure, skeeter pain.
The swans swim, the snipes soar,
Who could ever ask for more?
Between the bogs, trimmed by trees,
Fantastic Finland, sure to please.

*Crex is the genus of short-billed rails, semi-aquatic birds often difficult to find in their reedy marsh habitats

Redshank - Redshanks are long-legged shorebirds with red legs.

Streaky, spotty bird.
Wings are black and white.
Legs so long and red.
Such a pretty sight.

Wryneck - The Wryneck is an odd Old-World woodpecker *Jynx* is the species name.

A jynx at camouflage,
Unseen from below.
Hardly seems a bird.
Brown and strange and slow.

Smew - The Smew is a black-and-white duck found in Scandinavia and across Russia, as well as sometimes in Alaska.

Dazzling white and black,
Saucy snowy crown,
Eyepatch adds more class,
The female's grayish brown.

Siberian Tit (Gray-headed Chickadee) - The Siberian Tit, aka Gray-headed Chickadee, is a chickadee of Finland and Siberia, only found, with difficulty, in arctic North America.

Sometimes suet, sometimes seeds,
Flitting, hopping as it feeds,
Cap as gray as it can be,
Seems to be a chickadee.

Wide-billed Sandpiper

Legs are short,
Snipe-like crown,
Patterned back,
Bill turned down.

Yellow-billed Loon - These loons are the only loons with yellow bills. Like all loons they dive often and are usually underwater and invisible.

Disappearing bird,
Disappearing bill,
Seen upon a lake,
Causes quite a thrill.

Jaeger - Jaegers are brown gull-like birds that prey on other large birds and steal their food.

Speeding fighter plane,
Hurtling through the air,
Stealing from the terns,
Doesn't seem quite fair.

Finland Vignettes

Two Smew swiftly flew,
Spruce spires 'round me grew,
Sounds of swans filled the air;
Ruffled Ruffs* were everywhere.

*Ruffs are medium-sized shorebirds; the males have distinctive, often colorful, neck ruffs.

1999 – MIDWAY ISLAND

Midway Island was opened for a few years to nature-travelers. Around the old military buildings where we stayed were nearly a million Laysan Albatrosses, nesting on the ground, unafraid.

Tripping over albatrosses, monstrous gooney birds.
As far as I can see, they cover up the land.
An island where our people were never meant to be,
The birds have their traditions; they do not understand.

2000 - ISRAEL AND JORDAN (3/19-4/21/00)

This was another Massachusetts Audubon Society trip. While most of the people whom I know who have visited this part of the world did so for religious or historic reasons, of course, my visit was for the birds.

The Amazing Birds

A plurality of pipits, a wide swath of swifts,
A Holy Land journey the spirit uplifts.

A rapture of raptors, a kettle of kites,
Cetti's and Bluethroats and other delights.

A wringing of Wryneckss, a lyric of larks,
A blizzard of buzzards, the lights and the darks,

A wiggle of wagtails, and of wheatears, a sheaf,
And then the Sandgrouse – such a relief!

A surprise Little Owl perched on a post,
A stare of Stone-Curlews—those wanted most.

Unlimited Whitethroats, Chiffchaffs without end,
Buntings and finches as we ascend.

A hoopla of Hoopoes, a blackening of crows,
A storm cloud of storks, as the wind blows.

For each of the birders, an abundance of bliss
That birding can be as joyous as this.

Last Day in Israel (4/2/00)

'Twas the last day of Israel, and all through the plane,
The passengers dozed, enmeshed in their pain.

The suitcases stuffed by the travelers with care,
Accompanied their owners who flew through the air.

The birders were nestled un-snug in their seats,
While needles of sleepiness prickled their feets.

When what to my wondering eyes should appear,
But a video camera holding Anna*, so dear.

Her eyes were like sunshine, her smile made me sing,
Like flowers and dewdrops and birds on the wing.

And I heard me exclaim as we flew through the night,
"With this miracle baby, the world is all right!"

*the leader's daughter

2001 - THE PHILIPPINES

I went to the Philippine Islands with KingBird Tours. We sampled a few islands, saw many birds, and got rained on a lot.

Philippine Snapshot

The Philippines, a land of greens:
Palms, acacia, fields of rice.

Luzon hills, rocks and rills,
Endemic birds are very nice.

Waltzing through Luzon (tune: "Waltzing Matilda" – for Eric the Australian on the trip; leader Ben King)

Chorus: Birding with KingBird (3x); we see the birds (or we think that we do); shamas and shortwings, babblers and small things; y'all come along and you'll see them too.

Once a man named Ben took a group out to the Philippines, took them to the mountains and took them to the sea; everywhere they went there were birds beneath the underbrush; y'all come a-birding to Luzon with me. **Chorus.**

Then came the raptors, soaring o'er the mountain slopes, followed by owls hooting, one, two, three. Then the hanging-parrots, cuckoo-shrikes and cuckoo-doves; y'all come a-birding to Luzon with me. **Chorus.**

Up flew the sunbirds, up into the flowering tree, surrounded by flowerpeckers and white-eyes three. Lots of lovely birds to elate the rabid birding folks; y'all come a-birding to Luzon with me. **Chorus.**

Luzon Eagles

'Twas our Philippines trip and all through the bus,
Everything was rattling; it made such a fuss.

There was eagle-eye Eric, Bob and wife Ann;
Harriet; the punster, all on the plan.

When what to our wondering eyes should appear,
But a Philippine Hawk-Eagle; we saw it quite clear.

His tarsi, how feathered; his breast beige and brown,
His eyes kept a lookout, upward and down.

I slowly approached, with my camera took sight,
His beauty spread forth as he lifted in flight.

We boarded the bus, and our journey went on,
Exploring the wonders and thrills of Luzon.

Then toward the mountains, there arose a big bird;
His wings were immense, his size was absurd.

It was THE Eagle* – a spectacular feat;
Our trip 1/3 over, and yet 'twas complete!

*the Harpy Eagle, the goal of most birders who visit the Philippines

Furtive Flycatcher (the real name of this bird is the Furtive Flycatcher)

The furtive fly, the furtive fly;
it flits away in the blink of an eye.
And then I spy the furtive fly;
no happier person exists than I.

Palawan Trail – Melodious Babbler

I walk along the trail, my eyes alert and bright,
Expectant and excited, though there's not a bird in sight.

I know they're out there somewhere. I can hear the chirps and trills,
What's more, I have been promised that on this trip will be thrills.

Is that leaf really moving? Did a shadow just dart through?
Did I just glimpse a babbler? Was that the thing that flew?

It's there, and then it's vanished. Oops, it flew across the trail.
If I stare through that opening – surely, I'll not fail.

And then it sings behind me; the tape has lured it out.
Then there's five around me, and then I give a shout.

I see one really close, but of course, it plays its game.
Though only briefly viewed, it's a lifer just the same.

Philippines-Negros Island White-winged Cuckoo Shrike (tune: "Everything's Up to Date in Kansas City")

Everything's awful wet on Negros Island,
A tropical depression's got us down.
My boots are filled with water, as we slog the slippery trail,
We saw the cuckoo-shrike, but then my legs began to fail,
We played the tape for babblers, but to no avail.
We went about as fur as we could go,
And that's about as fur as I can go.

Bohol – Pitta, etc. (tune: "Over the River")

Over the river and through the woods, to Bohol we do go.
Our leader knows where the birds do repair
On ridges and outcrops, so…
Over the roots and the rocks and the mud,
The trogons and pittas we spy.
Hurrah for the hawk-cuckoo, the fruit-dove, the kite,
Hurrah for another white-eye.

Cebu Flowerpecker Watch

We passed on by the Mangrove Fly; we're bound for flowerpeckers in the sky.
We park ourselves on bamboo shelves and wait for little things to fly.
"Tea for two" sings the cuckoo; we wait another hour or two.
The coucal calls, as evening falls; bulbuls and drongos charge on through.
A pleasant day, that much I'll say, as the hours of waiting slipped away.
Flowerpeckers swift, a mini-gift; in days of sun, another ray.

Birding Philippines-Advice to a Novice

Do you want to know how it is to bird in the Philippine isles?
You take the very worst skulker that is and hide him behind brushy piles.
You color him brown with cute little stripes and place him in sun-dappled shade.
You roll the rocks in red mud, the slipperiest God ever made.
You hike through the forests and fields, o'er mountains and down rocky dales,
You bring on the clouds and the rain, making rivers where once there were trails,
You play a tape of his song, every fifteen minutes or so,
You squint and you peer, and you listen, and hope that the birdie will show.
Sometimes you do see the bird, and marvel that luck's come your way.
Quite often, however, you'll need to go looking on some other day.

Mindanao Medley (Philippines)

A maze of trails crosses the land,
From the distant sea to the hill where I stand.
The trees are tall, the canopy dense.
Our search for birds is quite intense.
A flock of white-eyes flutters by,
A fantail makes a distant cry.
A Hooded Sunbird probes the flowers.
We watch the eagle sit for hours.
McGregor's Cuckoo-Shrikes flock by.
The ibis forage against the sky.
The Apo Sunbird and the Myna.
Really nothing could be finer.
The Flowerpeckers and the Racquet-tails.
Against these wonders, all else pales.

Jeepney Exegesis
Much of the Philippine travel is by Jeepney, which I've tried to describe in this poem.

Poems in steel and paint they are,
Personalized with drivers' treasures.
Riding in one is another thing,
Not among life's greatest pleasures.

There's a cab in front where the driver sits,
With a holding tank attached to the rear.
A narrow bench is on each side,
With space beneath to stow some gear.

Windows run along the walls,
An open doorway at the back,
No shock-absorbers will you find,
A deeply regretted, tragic, lack.

Each bump and hole jolts every bone,
And bumps there are, and holes to spare.
When it rains, plastic curtains fall,
Shutting out the view – and air.

Yet all in all, a jeepney's good,
It gets one where one wants to be,
What it lacks in comfort, grace,
It makes up in efficiency.

Birding in the Rain (tune: "Just A-walking in the Rain")

Just a-birding in the rain, getting soaking wet,
Hoping the next bird will be the best one yet.

Just a-birding in the rain, deep within the trees,
Hoping that real soon there'll be a little breeze.

BIRDING TIMES, A LIFE IN RHYMES

Birds dart through the treetops, they just pass us by
Others squawk around us and make me want to cry.

Just a-birding in the rain, down a soggy slope,
Each time there's a bird, I feel a burst of hope.

Just a-birding in the rain, with a group of five,
Wondering if we will see a bird alive.

Just a-birding in the rain, not an end in sight,
Knowing that the birds will still turn out all right.

And So, It Goes...in the Philippines

There are birds for sale in the jungle.
There are birds being sold on the street.
There are trees being felled every minute.
There are rivers of mud 'neath my feet.
There are villages built on destruction,
An irreversible fate.
Shortsightedly gaining, but losing
The wonders that made their land great.

Ode to a Jeepney

A jeepney ride is a thing to behold,
a decorated steel design,
But young bones grow quickly old
with jolted back and bruised behind.
Whenever raindrops drench the land,
it keeps out rain, but also air.
It makes a rocky road from sand.
I feel each bump and hole that's there.

Under the Wire (tune: "I Want a Girl, Just Like the Girl")

I want a bird, just like the bird, that Ben said we would find,
A Wattled Broadbill up against the sky, one with blue encircled 'round his eye.

I want a bird, just like the bird…
He found it!

Wattled Broadbill

2002 – PERU (July 23- August 7)

I joined my NC birding friend Lena on a nature trip to Peru. Even the non-fanatic birdwatchers on the trip were overwhelmed by the beauty and number of birds.

With nature the theme, Peru was the dream,
We boarded the plane, our NC-based team.

With Cuzco the start, we each did our part,
Exploring the jungle, the rivers, the mart.

Cloud forest light, a misty delight,
Euphonias, tanagers, all things in flight.

Cocks-of-the Rock, flock after flock,
Birds always found when e'er we took stock.

Eagle and wren, tanagers again,
The days were quite pleasant, unstressful and then,

A bus, storm and rio, this was the trio,
That brought us, near-drowned, into the frio.

Boca Manu may mean nothing to you,
But it's where we turned north, our adventurous crew.

The weather was wet, quite depressing and yet,
We kept on aslogging; it was pointless to fret.

We found there were birds, too numerous for words,
And galloping peccaries, passing in herds.

Screaming macaws, caimen with jaws,
And a room-schedule system that had a few flaws.

To Machu Pichu by train, not one drop of rain,
A million steps climbed; our legs felt the pain.

Around us, the past, astounding and vast,
Glories and culture do not always last.

A Lima return, more time to burn,
And still stuff to buy around every turn.

Finally, the flight, delayed most the night,
Took us from darkness into the light.

2002- CALIFORNIA & ARIZONA (January)

In early 2003 I joined a Wings Birding Tours van trip that birded its way from the far west to Arizona. Not only do I do birding big years, but I also (at least I did at that time) eagerly keep track of birds that I have ever seen in the "ABA Area" – my life birds. As this trip began, I knew there was a chance that I could reach 700 for my ABA Area life list. And I did, in a destination spot teeming with thrashers. But it took a while:

LeConte's #700*

In the midst of a desert, the sage and the sand,
I've been running and 'scoping but now I just stand.

My throat is so dry; my feet are so tired,
But I'm beginning to feel amazed and inspired.

The Thrasher, LeConte's, a runner, so swift,
My one view, in flight, a surprising, quick gift.

700 I've seen, that's "ABA birds".
Elation flows o'er me, surrounding my words.

So, what will be next? The quest will not stop.
Either birds will run out, or I guess I'll just drop.

   *My life list of birds in the ABA Area reached 700 species with this LeConte's Thrasher.

Deserts in January

Deserts in Winter, a bird trip.
January, two thousand and two.
The trip is a great one, and birdy,
And the people are wonderful too.

John, the tender of bird life.
Susan, tending phone at his side.
Carl, who's filming the whole thing.
Kirk, absent-minded with pride.

Burt, who keeps us all guessing.
Dorothy, with raven-black hair.
Alice, a bit quiet and serious.
Lois, you know that she's there.

And then there is Sue, she's my roommate,
Cheerful and bouncy and all.
At last, we come to our leader,
Bird-finder, extraordinaire, Paul.

Thrashers, gnatcatchers, sparrows,
Towhees, blackbirds and quail,
Raptors, hummers and wrens,
He's found them all without fail (nearly).

Canyon Towhee

Sue's Song (tune: "In a Canyon")

In a canyon, is a towhee, and it's waiting just for me.
I will find that little skulker, said my roommate Sue to me.

Brown it was and like a field mouse, lurking shy beneath a tree,
But it hopped out and we saw it. That's the end of this story.

Baird's Sparrow Lament (Tune: "Mine Eyes Have Seen the Glory…")

Mine eyes have seen a flock of larks. I've seen my share of quails.
I've seen pipits, I've seen meadowlarks, I even have seen rails.
I've seen soaring hawks, and diving ducks, but before my eyesight fails,
I want to see a Baird's.
Glory, glory, what a great trip we have had.
Glory, glory, just to leave it makes me sad.
Glory, glory, there is naught I want so bad,
As to keep on tromping for Baird's.

2002– CUBA (January)

In order to travel to Cuba from the United States, we needed to be part of a bird "survey team," which our Massachusetts Audubon trip officially was.

Survey Theme/Cheer

Leave by dawn, survey on; survey team hurray!
Forth we sally, keeping tally, survey team, olé.
Bouncing bus, lots of fuss; survey team hurray
Through the "winder", naught shall hinder; survey team, olé.

What's the hurry? What, me worry? survey team hurray
Need to tree 'em, and to see 'em; survey team, olé.
Sounds we're hearing, trogons nearing; survey team hurray.
Tody, Flicker, counting quicker; survey team, olé.
Numbers mounting, still we're counting; survey team hurray.
We're what we seem – a survey team; survey team, olé.

Cuban Tody

2002 – SICHUAN CHINA (April 29-May 27)

This was another KingBird Tours trip.

Sichuan

Who is that masked man? Why, I believe it's Ben
Leading a group to Sichuan again.
The time – it is May of 2002, and
Not having anything better to do,
I had joined with the birders, bound for the hills,
Looking, once more, for Mr. King's "thrills".
We first went to Wolong, the home of the panda.
We laboriously climbed a large mountain, and a
Great place it turned out to be,
For pheasants and warblers and tits in the trees.
As we drove to the pass, the world turned to snow,
With monals and partridges above and below.
And then we turned north to the high endless plains,
Land of the skylarks, ground tits and cranes,
Yaks wandering everywhere, roads full of holes,
Marmots and pikas and sakers on poles.
The road to Ju-jai-go, and the nearby reserve,
I'll never forget, nor did I deserve.
But inside the reserve, Chinese thrushes were found,

Rosefinches in bushes and grouse on the ground.
A day full of Galliformes –partridge and pheasant,
In spite of the cloudiness, really quite pleasant.
I'll not dwell on the hours spent on the robin,
But the other new birds kept me from sobbin'.
And then we turned south,to where we'd begun,
A trip full of wonder, exertion and fun.

Yaks (and a Birder's Plea) (tune: "Don't Fence Me In")

Oh, give me yaks, lots of yaks, across the vast Tibetan plains,
They're not fenced in.
See them graze 'til the grass disappears beneath the ground,
They're not fenced in.
See them run o'er the hills that are decimated,
'til all the living things are extirpated,
Just thinking 'bout it gets me all agitated,
Please fence them in.

Forced Marches

Bus stops, driver scowls.
No, it's not a stop for owls.
Door opens, out we go,
In the mud or in the snow.
Slogging upward, lacking air,
Something here is not quite fair,
Bus is gone, out of sight.
Will we have to spend the night?
Around the curve, where's the bus?
He's not waiting there for us!
Our smoking driver, we finally see.
Is it for this we've paid a fee?

Favorite Things (tune: "Favorite Things")

Crag Martins swooping 'round steep rocking crags,
Lammergeiers soaring, a wagtail that wags,
Cranes flying low with the sun on their wings,
These are a few of my favorite things.

When the phone trills, when I pay bills, when I'm feeling stressed, I
simply remember my favorite things, and then I feel very blessed.

Small buffy warblers that all look the same,
Firethroats aglowing and woodpeckers, tame,
Fulvettas with splashes of orange on their wings,
These are a few of my favorite things.

Snow on the mountains and snow in the passes
Larks flying high o'er the vast plains of grasses,
Snowcocks on mountains, such happiness bring,
These are a few of my favorite things.

Bouncing Bus Ride (tune: "Raindrops Keep Falling on My Head")

Noodles keep falling on my head, and
Just when I think the road is going to level out,
Here comes an orange,
Nothing's fastened down,
Boxes all around,
Tripods crashing to the ground,
And there's one thing I know.
The boxes though they get me, may have chocolate,
So, I'll just go and bird tomorrow.

Ferruginous Flycatcher

The ferruginous fly, the ferruginous fly.
He appeared one day, and a witness was I,
With his charcoal moustaches and little white chin,
An appearance calculated to make me grin,
Eyes white-encircled; ever-moving rufescence,

A small slice of lively bright effervescence.

Ferruginous Flycatcher

Black-necked Crane (tune: "The Rain in Spain...")

The crane, not in vain, we found mainly on the plain.
In Taiwan, Hong Kong and Wolong, Gruidae hardly happen.
Once again, we found the crane, with no pain, without rain,
And where's that glorious crane? On the plain, on the plain.

Sichuan Collage

Rivers rushing, dippers dipping,
Birders climbing, some are slipping.
Skulkers skulking, firethroats firing,
Golly this can be quite tiring.
Warblers warbling, kites are kiting,
Actually, this is quite exciting.
Redstarts starting, swallows swallowing,
Now it's in the mud we're wallowing.
Pheasants crowing-there's a switch.
Now we've got to cross a ditch.
Babblers babbling, swifts are swifting.
This part's gotten quite uplifting.
Laughingthrushes laughing, wagtails wagging.
Now it seems the group is dragging.
The bus and days descend and ascend,
Over and over until the end.

2003 – ECUADOR

This was a very good Field Guides trip to a very birdy country.

On the Plane (1/25/03)

Morosely my mind meanders, me thinks.
My eyes slowly closing in widely spaced blinks.
The plane jiggles on, from the north to the south.
The taste of the chicken recedes from my mouth.
I worry and wonder each time that I fly –
Will this be the trip on which I will die?
I've too many things that I still plan to do.
Of all of my lists I've accomplished so few.
I pray in my soul, please spare me for now.
I'll try, I'll do better, I promise, I vow.

January 2003 Birding Nightmare

'Twas in the month of Enero, in the year 2003,
When I swear I heard the leader say urgently to me,
"It's a Carbonated Wisteria – it's right behind that limb"
I knew the chance of seeing it was extraordinarily slim.
The rain was pouring steadily, the leaves were broad and dense,
The days of ruthless birding, exceedingly intense.
Already we had seen the Nobulated Brat,
the Yellow-toenailed Tree-Blob, the Greenish Barfing Chat,
This bird it seemed to jump around, with movement here, then there,
But alas 'twas only raindrops. It really wasn't fair.
I tried in vain to see it. I squinted and I stared.
Everyone tried to help me, but finally I despaired.
I just gave up and moaned aloud, which woke me up real fast.
A travelling birder's nightmare – the ghost of birding past.

BIRDING TIMES, A LIFE IN RHYMES

Ode to Field Guides (tune: "Swing Low, Sweet Chariot") (2/1/03)

Look low. Look down for the bird, skulking up the slippery slope.
Look high – there goes the bird, but I do not give up hope.
I looked over the agave, and what did I see sitting on the little bent twig,
A Loja hummer staring at me, made me want to do a little jig.

Walk down, walk down through mud, listening for a flock to come by,
Walk up, and follow the leader, looking for a bird in the sky.
I heard squawking parakeets and what did I see, way down the valley below?
A pair of parakeets coming straight to me, made me glad that I had spent the dough.

Drive down, drive down the road, heading north for little flying things.
Drive up, up toward the clouds, just as if our arms had turned to wings.
I looked out the window and what did I see, lots of birds for which I had no name,
But there was help right beside me. I am very glad that I came.

Time for Birds (2/7-10/03)

The windows are fogged; no one can see out.
The rain's pouring down, but still, I don't pout,
For we've seen many hummers, just hours ago.
And two strolling Seedsnipe were right down below.
The days have been filled (partly with rain),
And the ears of our leaders have brought us much gain.
Tiny tyrannulets; piculets perky,
Colorful trogons, antbirds quite murky,
Flocks of flycatchers, creepers and gleaners,
Tapaculos and antwrens with their skulking demeanors.
Aracaris and toucans, breathtaking sights,
The tanager flocks, most welcome delights.
Some tanagers' colors have shouted aloud,
While others, more somber, have hid under shroud.
The swordbills and Sylphs with their elongated parts

Have brought light to our eyes and joy to our hearts.
So now that I've finished this page full of words,
I think I see sun – it's time for more birds!

2013 – HONDURAS (2/21)

A trip to Honduras; it's been very long
Since I've flown off to bird, to hear southern bird song.
To immerse myself, capture the beauty of birds,
At the end to bring home what says more than words.

PELAGIC TRIPS

The word "pelagic" is probably not in many non-birder vocabularies, but for birders, especially fanatic birders, it is well-known. A pelagic trip for birders is a boat trip on a large body of water, generally on the ocean, far from land, designed to find seabirds, many of which are rarely visible from land (other than from distant islands). Birders need to go on pelagic trips if they want to add pelagic birds to their bird life-lists or their year-lists. I do not know how to swim and was afraid I would go overboard on ocean birding trips when the waves were rough. In my earlier days of pelagic birding, I was also often seasick until I concocted my own remedies.

Pre-Pelagic Jitters (9/13/97)

I'm in a motel room near the New Jersey coast,
At the end of a day of driving and birds.
I'm facing another – doing what I love most,
But it's out on the ocean, too scary for words.

It's highly unlikely there'll be anything new,
And my stomach will probably bubble, be riled,
Yet I'm brimming with joy, not at all blue,
A day out with nature and elements wild.

Today on the ferry from Del. to Cape May,
I pictured ice bergs and penguins ahead –
A bigger adventure that's coming my way*,
Looked to with joy, punctured by dread.

Afraid of the waves and unending seas,
No way to escape, once it's begun,
Balancing pleasure with quavering knees,
Hoping that misery is outweighed by fun.

The promise of time with new friends and old,
Looking for birds, where we've not ever been—
A likely addiction, so I've been told, --
At theme oft repeated, again and again.

*on an upcoming Antarctica trip; not on this pelagic trip.

Ocean Travel to the Dry Tortugas (4/29/01)

Up, crash! Down!
Shiver all around.
Waves splashing over us.
On our way to town.

Stomachs jolt and heave,
So hard to believe.
That a good bird going by us
Would misery relieve.

Faces wan and pale,
Clinging to a rail,
Praying that the boat
Will not go down or fail.

The birds must cross it too
Without a boat or crew.
I don't know how they do it-
Explains why there's so few.

The birds must dread the flying
And face the trip with sighing.
Too bad that we can't help them,
And keep them all from dying.

First Pelagic Trip of the Year (6/17/05)

The waves stretch forever, way out of sight,
Spangled with seaweed, and froth-tipped in white.
Normally I'd feel uncomfortable and queasy,
But the birds today have been wonderful, easy.
A couple Masked Boobies before we half knew it,
A Tropicbird, Red-billed, that flew (it
Circled the boat giving great views to all),
And two kinds of Storm-Petrels; 'twas Overton's call.
Great schools of tuna, and a whale-shark, seen twice.
Sooty and Bridled Terns – really quite nice,
Shearwaters: Audubon's, a Cory's also.
Things came, 'cross the waves, above and below.

The Second (of Five) Texas Pelagics (7/28/05)

Now there's little that rhymes with "pelagic", unless you consider the magic
Of the birds yet to be and a day on the sea, a day that, of course, is not tragic.
Another bird seen that I needed, and it was Mike Overton who ID'd it,
As we coursed through the waves, on a bright glorious day, as onward our fishing boat speeded.
Now the birds on the Gulf are quite scattered, but of course that's not ever mattered,
All I need is a new one, an out-of-the-blue one, and my faith in pelagics unshattered.
And then there's the matter of whales, besides which a storm-petrel pales,
Over ten, they were sperm, a taxonomic term, and probably most were females.

A pelagic goes on to its ending, my energy levels descending,
But I am no fool, pelagics are cool, three more, I'll of course be attending.

September Pelagic (9/17/05)

It was dark out there, the sea blue-black.
If not for my big year, I might've wanted to go back.
Peter, Eric, Brad, John and Dwight –
Our leaders were poised as we plunged through the night.
The day dawned with no birds around,
But we kept on going to where we were bound.
A Tropicbird again broke the monotony,
As the water got deeper, and clouds got less cottony.
For two Frigatebirds we finally then dashed,
As over us birders the waves wetly crashed.
The rest, they were great, but sadly, none new,
Cory's, Bridled, and Red-necked too.*
This pelagic trip was less birdy than some,
But not to take all would be just plain dumb.
Until you have gone and done the whole thing,
There's no way to know what a pelagic will bring.
PS. These trips were arranged by Sumita Prasad.
So, thanks to her, the leaders and God.
That's the way it goes in a big year in September.
It's hard to imagine the coming December.

*Shearwater, Tern and Phalarope, respectively

Pelagic Cancelled (10/8/05)

Driving along; Simone is asleep.
I hope the birds on the waters will keep.
Pelagic trip's cancelled, so where should we bird?
We keep checking emails, but nothing we've heard.
We checked out a gull, but a Laughing it was,
So, we're now heading west. The reason? Because
We love to buy gas and drive toward the sun
On long lines of pavement. Gosh this is fun!

Actually, it's titmice, nuthatches and such,
Right now, each new one is worth very much.
So onward we steam, not in our right minds,
Heading toward, hopefully, wondrous bird finds.

Another Pelagic Cancelled (10/21/05)

This time we went west *before* the pelagic,
Which also might cancel, and that might be tragic.
This time we actually made it to the Guads*,
And a Pygmy Nuthatch was produced by the gods.
Of course, that was after a very long climb,
Up to the Bowl, for the third time.
So, at least sometimes persistence pays.
You just gotta keep trying for days and days.

*Guadalupe Mountains of west Texas

Last Pelagic (11/5/05)

The waves were as forecast, six feet, maybe more.
We kept keeping on, distinctly hard-core.
At the back of the boat, I provided the chum,
So wobbly my knees, the rest of me numb.
Two more jaegers we saw, completing the set,
But my fear of the waves was not over yet.
If the truth could be known, I wanted to die,
But I wouldn't have seen the jaegers fly by.
No gain without pain, 'tis trite but 'tis true.
I rejoice in the gain. As for pain, I came through.
It's a story to tell when I'm older and grayer.
Not now on the sidelines – now I'm actually a player! *

*According to my calculations, this trip put my big year numbers at 511, which tied the previous Texas big year record. My final number for the year was 522.

Big Year Years

For fanatic, nutty, or otherwise obsessive birders, doing a big year comes quite naturally; however, for "normal" birders, big years are never attempted. My definition of a big year is that it is a year, normally chosen to begin on January 1st, during which the birder tries to see as many species of birds as possible in a chosen geographic area. Typically, that area is a county or a state, or for the most hardcore, a country, or the world. As summarized below, I have done state big years in Texas (twice: in 2003 and 2005), South Dakota (2012), Alaska (2016) and Wisconsin (2022). In addition, I have done a couple of county big years in Pennington County (SD). I also have done an "ABA big year," which when I did it in 2008, included the continental US and Canada and adjacent ocean waters, but not Hawaii (Hawaii was added to the definition of an ABA big year after 2008). My total for that year was 723 bird species. The following poems relate primarily to big year adventures that were not on the ocean, most ocean-related birding poems being included in the pelagic birding section.

A Summary of My Big Years (12/26/21)

Just about nineteen years ago,
Doing a "big year" was not on my mind.
I thought I would just wander around Texas,
And see just how many birds I could find.

Texas has 254 counties,
And I had already birded in most of the state.
In '03 I birded nearly every county
Getting up early and staying up late.

To my amazement when '03 was over
My tally of birds was really quite high.
It got me to thinking: could I do a "real" big year?
Be intentional? Give it a try?

LYNN E. BARBER

So, in '04 I rested, staying out of the race,
Thought about where I would bird, if I tried,
Studied my bird books and looked at the maps,
And in '05 I launched it – serious – statewide.

It turned out that in '05 in Texas,
Many birds were surprising, unexpected and rare.
I raced to the south, to the east, west and north,
And mostly I found the birds that were there.

I broke all the records, a BIG year it was,
Then a friend gave me a book, *The Big Year*
About birding obsessively all over the country,
Taking big year birding to a whole higher tier.

My heart starting racing – such an adventure,
But I knew it would take so very much money.
The cost calculations to bird the whole country
Were beyond laughable, not even funny.

My big year aspirations were tamped down. I rested.
But then started figuring how to reduce the spending
Of doing a very, very, very big year –
Lots of cost-cutting and travel-amending.

I started in Texas, which I knew very well,
My "ABA big year" that I did in '08.
Multiple trips to each coast and the sea.
Nonstop birding from state to state.

I managed to find over 700 species,
The first woman to do that, I guess.
It was costly, exhausting, miraculous, amazing.
Was I glad that I did it? Certainly! Yes!

After a few years we moved to South Dakota:
Lots of neat birds, a new world to explore.

South Dakota is smaller than Texas.
A big year might be easier than those done before.

It was, and I did it, another big year,
Criss-crossing the state, to and fro, fro and to.
When 2012 ended, three others and I
Had exceeded the past, with little to rue.

In 2013 I did a county big year,
And then another, overlappingly so.
And then we were gone to Alaska.
Should I do another? Definitely no!

Of course, by 2016, I was at it again,
Flying to islands and the frozen north land:
An Alaska big year, astoundingly different
Than what I had previously worked on or planned.

In 2021 we moved to Wisconsin.
Now – it's nearly a new year, about on the brink,
Wondering whether I'll do another.
I don't know. Will I? What do you think?

Big Year Patience (2/18/22)

One waits and waits and waits some more.
I guess that's what a big year's for.
Patience – for which I truly yearn.
Patience – that I've yet to learn.

Texas (2003 and 2005)

Searching for Birds (written during my first sort-of big year in Texas) (12/1/03)

I hurry, I drive, I eat up the miles-
I race and I see! And I'm nothing but smiles.

Another day's racing, and nothing I see,
But the search must go on, whatever will be.

If I don't make the effort, don't go for the chance,
I'm not with the program, not dancing the dance.

It's like life at its essence, if one doesn't try,
One is left in the dirt, never glimpses the sky,

Never tastes all the flavor, never feels, does not give,
Never breathes in God's blessings or learns how to live.

Big Year Words of Wisdom (2003)

These words of wisdom are
    for those who think a big year might be fun.
A big year birding is not just
    some gentle birding in the sun.

Be sure your loved ones and your job
    can spare your presence many days.
Be sure your rain gear and your car
    are there for you without delays.

You better not procrastinate,
    the bird you want will fly away.
Do not delay; do not wait;
    it won't be seen another day.

Be willing to receive some tips
> as well as kind advice.
Do not for one minute believe
> your efforts alone will suffice.

Do not despair if you miss birds,
> or there are birds you can't ID.
Life will go on, and there is this:
> rejoice in those that you DID see!

Put aside your conscience,
> invest instead in Mobil, Exxon, BP, Shell.
The gas you use will be enough
> to get from home (and back) to Hell.

You'll spend more hours on the road,
> than in the woods or at the beach,
But you must keep driving 'cause you know
> your grasp will not exceed your reach.

Curse the wind and curse the rain,
> but bird you must, in spite of them.
Curse the hot and curse the ice.
> You gotta bird, though it's not nice.
Curse the year, yes, it will end,
> though likely you'll do it all again.

Heading Out Birding Near the End of 2003

Where's my diet drink? Where's my granola bar?
Where are my binoculars? Where's my trusty car?

Though normal folks sleep in comfort still,
I have beat the dawn, seeking one more thrill.

One more time, I hit the road. Only four more days to go.
I love it still, I cannot wait, though what I'll see I do not know.

On Big Year 2003 (1/11/04)

It got me to camp; it got me to climb.
It got me to bird 'most all of the time.

It got me to hear; it got me to see.
It made my life buoyant, exciting and free.

It drove me to drive every road of this state.
It got me up early and kept me up late.

You ask if I'd do it all over again.
Don't ask me "if"; just ask me "when."

Big Year Again, Texas (2005)

I'm doing it again, said the birder to the list.
Every bird in Texas, 'cept the ones that will be missed.

Missed Bird (2005)

You heard the word – absurd! The bird
It flew! So blue. Curfew, for you.

St. David (3/1/05) Dave is my loving, non-birding spouse, who somehow seems to understand my birding mania.

St. David – how apt the name: he lets me bird my fill.
He lets me wander to and fro and do just what I will.
He doesn't squawk, when I announce, "They've found another bird."
When I depart, he says, "Good by", without another word.

Five Months into My Texas Big Year (5/30/05)

The problem with driving across this broad state,
Is that it gives me time to contemplate
The idiocy of the five months past,
And seven more! I hope I last.
With each bird reported not yet on my list,
I must hop in my car – it can't be missed!

The miles fly by, as do the birds.
It really is too nuts for words.
Yet there's an odd pleasure as the total rises,
Filled with wondrous, bizarre surprises,
With "easy" birds that can't be found,
But rarities that much abound.
No one could've predicted what's happened to date,
Nor what would be my big year's fate.
Let's hope it's not what happened to my car,
Which died from being driven too far.
Let's hope that birds keep being spotted,
That t's are crossed, and i's are dotted,
That migrants are manifest, and days are long,
That snows are early, and fronts are strong.
That I hold out and my new car does too,
That finds are many and misses are few,
As I roam the state both far and near,
And that there's time to sleep in the coming year.

Planning Big Year Birding in Texas (9/1/05)

I kept hitting the books again and again,
On where to find birds, and critically, when?
Should I go west to the mountains or south to the Valley?
Should I cover each lake, or check someone's alley?
After thinking it over, I'd draw up a plan,
But then realize once I began,
That birds in many cases hadn't done the same reading.
They were off somewhere else, sleeping or feeding.
The real challenge was: to think like a bird,
But birdbrains are small, so that was absurd.
So, I often just winged it, appropriate, I guess.
Would I do it again? The answer is "Yes!"

Pointless (10/4/05)

Pointless this trip,
Pointless it seems.
The point, however
Is clear in my dreams.

Near the End (11/25/05)

'Twas the end of November, big year near its end.
I thought of petitioning to make it extend.
The birds were all listed with care on the web.
Sightings were certainly stuck at an ebb.
Bird books still nestled in the back of my RAV
Showing the missing, the hoped for, the have,
While I with my camera and my warm fuzzy hat
Was trying to decide, should I chase this or that?
[not finished]

Near the End (12/12/05)

I look on the posts and the poles,
I look on the hills and in holes,
I look in the air,
And I look over there.
I might just see one of my goals.

Somewhere a bird lurks that is new
That will stand the test, tried and true,
But the year's nearly past,
And time's going fast.
There's only so much I can do.

Possibly there'll be a new one
Before my big year is all done,
Or perhaps two, or three,
Whatever will be,
But hasn't it really been so fun?

Closer to the End (12/20/05)

I'm driving home near the end of December.
I've been driving since – I can't remember.
The sky is gray, my mood is bleak.
For three days not finding the bird* I seek.
I could give up and call it quits,
But not going birding gives me fits.
I wonder, when this year has ended,
Will my whole life just be suspended?
Will I withdraw, a shamble, quaking?
It will be tough, there's no mistaking.
But for now, I must keep trying,
Don't want to end the year with crying.
I need another, a grand finale.
'twould make the holidays most jolly.
Eleven days are left and so,
It won't be long before I go
Out to find what I can find
(I'll worry later 'bout losing my mind).

*Thick-billed Kingbird

Christmas Texas Snow (12/25/05) My last big birding trip in 2005 was to find a female Snow Bunting (my sketch is of a male), not rare but very unusual for Texas, especially south Texas, that someone had reported on South Padre Island on December 24th. People who went to see her found her on a well-mowed lawn in an RV park, often hopping around, next to an old anchor, staying in the shade.

Little Snow Bunting, got sick of the cold,
So, she headed south, out of the fold.
She kept on going, the world was all changed.
She was beginning to feel a bit deranged.
And then she finally found a shore.
She really couldn't fly anymore.
She fluttered down, sore to the bone,
And by George*, it looked like a home.
The birders came from far away
To see this bird on Christmas Day.
Around her little anchor bed,
They scattered seeds, and she was fed.

*Thanks to George and Scarlet and all those who cared for her

What Do You Need to Do a Big Year? (12/26/05)

So, what do you need to do a big year?
You need boundless energy and a minimum of fear.
Auto insurance and a sturdy car,
Which without complaining will travel far.
And which you aren't afraid will get dirty or marred,
And money for gas, and a good credit card.
Binoculars, of course, and a camera that you
Can show the world what you saw too.
You need a life that is droppable when that email arrives,
And a tolerance for sitting and long boring drives.
A resilient spirit when the birds you chase
Just vanish. Poof! With nary a trace.
You need a love of listing and numbers and tally.
A body, which sleepless, continues to rally.
The ability to drive as if blinders you wear,
Not looking here or stopping there,
Yet at the same time, knowing when you should stop,
Knowing which plans to follow and which you should drop.
Bird books (that's plural) and the ability to use them
To identify birds and (hopefully) not confuse them.
Almost forgot sunscreen and bug-spray and maps,

And a good pair of glasses to watch for speed-traps.
Of course, you need birds to arrive in the state
That will time their arrival not too early or late,
Especially you need the surprising and rare
To augment the birds that ought to be there.
The willingness to accept: not all birds that you see
Can be counted by you; it ain't meant to be.
In fact, there'll be birds that you'd swear were pure gold
That are questionable or hybrids (or so I've been told).
And you need helpful people who will email and call
And will be out there birding to assist in your "haul".
A way for people to contact you when
You're miles from civilization and then
The will to drag yourself back on the road
In the opposite direction, or, from your abode.
A village is actually what you require
To get all the birds to which you aspire.
And most of all a love of birds,
That cannot, really, be conveyed in words.
And, if you are married, a spouse who will be
Astoundingly supportive, and who will really see
That this is the time that you just must spend,
And the year, eventually, certainly, will end.
Of course, all of these things might not even apply.
The bottom line – just give it a try!

The End (12/31/05)

It's over. It's finished. It's done. I'm through.
Though I'm glad it's over, am I sad? That too.
In fact, right now, I'm mostly sad.
Just think of all the fun I've had!
The miles that were driven, the birds that appeared,
An incredible, astounding, great big big year!
You might be asking, what happens after?
Well, for starters, lots of laughter.
A celebration of what occurred,
A great rejoicing in each little bird.

Then, lots of thanks to one and all
Who helped, encouraged, gave me a call.
Now it's your turn – get out there and look!
But as for me, I'm writing a book.

Obsessing about Doing (and Doing) an ABA Big Year (2006-2008)

Thoughts about Doing an ABA Big Year

In 2008, the "ABA Area" was defined to include the continental United States and Canada, and ocean waters up to 200 miles away or halfway to another country (it did not include Hawaii, which was added later). So doing an ABA big year meant seeing how many birds one could see in the ABA Area in one year. After I'd read Mark Obmascik's book, *The Big Year*, in 2006, which I was originally afraid to read because of what I knew it would do, I became convinced that I too needed to do an ABA big year. After calculating the likely cost I realized that it was not a rational, or even feasible, possibility. Thus, when 2007 began I did *not* begin such a year. As the year went on, however, I realized that I could do it less expensively, and so in 2008, I did.

Wishing for an ABA Big Year Before I Did One (3/16/06)

A Big Year I want, across this broad land,
But the money's not there, 'though the thing's mostly planned.
I'd go to Alaska, many times through the year.
I'd go on pelagics, though they fill me with fear.
I'd go up north owling, and south to the Keys.
I'd go up the east coast and walk through the trees.
I'd go to the Valley, climb up to Boot Springs.
I'd haunt Arizona for hummingbird wings.
I'd explore California along its long coast.
I'd go to the Gulf. I'd swelter and roast.
Of course, I'd come home, now and then for my work,
But most of the time I'd bird like berserk.

The Year after a Very Big Record-breaking Year in Texas (5/20/06)

It's not the same. I can't deny
That the big year thing gave me quite a high.
This year, when birding, although it's still fun,
Something in me wants to run,
Wants the pressure, wants to chase,
Wants the challenge and the race.
Is there a cure for big-year-it is?
A way to clear out this detritus?
I need to pause, and to remember,
It will not matter if, at the end of December,
There are birds I've not seen or bothered to chase
(that's assuming, of course, I'm still in first place).

Ten Months from a Possible ABA Big Year (2/10/07)

Arms akimbo; I'm in a limbo.
Ten more months, or slightly more.
Wanting chasing, heart a-racing,
Yet here I sit, feet on the floor.

Of course I'm reading, bird books heeding,
Trying to prepare my brain.
I try to learn it, yet I spurn it,
Sitting still is such a pain.

Deeply sighing, without crying,
I turn my mind to things mundane,
Like buying socks and travel clocks,
And things to keep off sun and rain.

It's odd, this waiting, though frustrating,
Also makes my spirits quicken.
Time for dreaming (while I'm scheming)
While I watch the clock keep ticking.

Niggling Worry (3/11/07)

Deep inside there's this niggling worry,
That if I do it, I'll really be sorry.
That I'll wreck my health and break the bank,
Be worn and haggard and a grumpy old crank.
Of course, that all might come to be,
But think of all the birds I'll see!
The sheer elation, the year-long high.
I need to do it before I die.
It's going to be tough, no easy pickin'
I'm surely not a springtime chicken.
But what I lack in youth and dough,
I hope I have in get-up-and-go.

Facing the Big Year (12/26/07)

It's nearing. Am I ready? Probably not. Who can tell?
Will it be like a whirlwind, or delirium, or hell?
Will I survive the intensity, the mania, the despair,
The need to find a bird that simply isn't there?
I need to take a deep breath, to think of what it means,
To realize that what I'm doing is only done in dreams.
To take the time to live what will surely be unique,
That half the fun is seeking, not just finding what I seek.
To live in every moment, though I'm planning far ahead,
To face it with excitement (and minimize the dread),
To know that when it's over, when all is said and done,
It won't be worth a nickel, if it isn't full of fun.
["Amen!" stated 1/23/08]

333* (1/31/08)

Three hundred and thirty-three:
A magical number, it seems to me.
Anyone else with sufficient obsessing
Could have done the same thing without even stressing.
I'm sure I'm nuts, but that's not new.
This is just something I have to do.

*The number of species I saw in my first month of my ABA big year

Driving (2/14/08)

Why are my poems so oft about driving,
Instead of the birds for which I am striving?
Because the driving is often so boring,
I need to do something to keep me from snoring,
And because when I'm birding, my thoughts do not stray
To plans for the future or things far away.
And so, the doggerel flows out of my pen,
And the miles are traversed, 'til I'm home again.

Am I Nuts? (2/24/08)

I've driven myself; I know it's true,
But there's so much I need to do.
Really it is in my head,
When everything is done and said.
Yet it's as if an outside hand,
Something I just don't understand,
Has hold of me and won't let go,
Is keeping me from going slow,
Is dragging me, is pushing, pulling,
It's not as if that I'm not willing,
But somehow, I must pause enough
To do the usual, mundane stuff,
To breathe, relax, regroup, repair,
And then find birds without despair.

Common Crane Chase in Nebraska (3/11/08)

There's a glimmer of hope that the crane is still there.
It just didn't put its head in the air.
Perhaps it is grazing, Sandhills all around.
Perhaps it wants by me to be found.
I've 200 miles left to drive.
I hope the crane is still alive.
In any case, the chase is on.

I hope the crane is not gone.
([it apparently WAS gone, and I did not find it)

Green-breasted Mango* Miracle in Georgia (3/24/08)

Slightly scimitrical bill,
Body of pulsating green,
Throat of a hue,
So stunning and true,
The purplist that I've ever seen.

Body and wings that are big,
Tail that is coppery and bold,
A most welcome sight,
In strong brassy flight,
A miracle to behold!

*a hummingbird that is a rare visitor to the United States from Mexico

Birder Gambling (4/2/08)

A big year quest is just like gambling –
You pays your money and then get rambling.
You takes your chances, and bet on winning,
But you also know, from the beginning,
That you might just never get what you're after,
Or maybe the day will end with laughter.
The birds will show, or they'll disappear.
The clouds will rain, or perhaps they'll clear.
You might get lucky, or lose the hand,
In spite of all you've done and planned.
You keep on trying; you keep obsessing,
You pray for yet another blessing.
The dice are thrown; the wheel is turning,
You hold your breath, are pulled by yearning.
You can't escape it, despite the cost,
Despite the hours of sleep you've lost.
The joker's you, but you're not knowing,

With blinders on, you keep on going.
Although you're doing something mad,
You do know that your heart is glad.
Yet big year birding's so much more:
It's peering out an open door
To see the beauty, hear the sound,
Of such a wondrous world around.

On the Road to Home (5/5/08)

The sky's cold and gray, the road rainy, wet.
My bank account's empty, and I'm deep in debt.

My head's feeling fuzzy, packed tightly with fog,
And sinking so slowly through a dark soggy bog.

My eyes are so tired, my shoulders so sore,
My thoughts stuffed with birds I don't need any more.

And with others that just refused to be found,
That hid in the bushes not making a sound.

This portrait I've painted, unfortunate but true,
Is not the full picture of what I'm going through.

This big year has actually <u>almost</u> always been fun,
In spite of the fact that I've stayed on the run.

But now, in between, removed from the highs,
Exclamations of joy are replaced by deep sighs.

I think I'll have time, soon, for sleep and for rest.
I'll need them of course to finish this quest.

Together with willpower and drive and caffeine,
I hope they will take me through times yet unseen.

So that when this year's over, this will just be a blip
On an otherwise magical, marvelous trip.

Adak (5/14/08)

I wonder as I wander o'er Adak's brown hills,
Will we ever find all our sought-after thrills?

Why I Shouldn't be Doing a Big Year (5/26/08)

The most obvious thing is the money it takes,
To fly hither and yon, to rent motels and cars,
To pay for the gas, the meals, the mistakes,
The sum of it all has just gone through the stars.

And then there's the worries that the plans will fall through,
Or the planes will fall down, or the luggage get lost,
Or the birds will not show, or I won't have a clue,
Of what I am seeing. Did I mention the cost?

And of course, there's my phobias and gut-wrenching fears,
As we bump through the skies in a sardine-can plane,
I think about upcoming rafting with tears,
And I watch all that dough as it swirls down the drain.

Do you notice a theme here? I'm sure that's the case-
The horrendous expense is getting me down!
Yet my worrying leaves when I enter the chase,
And a smile of delight replaces the frown.

Anwar (ANWR) (6/21/08)
The Alaska National Wildlife Refuge is over 19 million acres on Alaska's North Slope.

Millions and millions of acres, and miles of rivers than wind,
A refuge of breathless proportions, a gem and one of a kind.

With grizzlies and Dall sheep and eagles, rocky spires and green mossy rises,
And hidden in thick willow clusters, one of nature's tiniest surprises.

A chickadee*, small and gray headed, flitting constantly, feeding its young.
I sing of the need to preserve it – a song that I know must be sung.

*The Gray-headed Chickadee, previously called the Siberian Tit. In the United States it is only found in a tiny area in far northern Alaska.

Mid-year Cogitations (6/23/08)

I could not see the forest or trees,
'til I went north to seek chickadees.
Now the whole thing is clear,
And sadly, I fear
That I'm killing myself by degrees.

There is something bizarre and absurd
About living one's life just to bird.
There's no rudder, no balance,
No skills and no talents,
Yet this mania cannot be deterred.

Don't ask if it makes any sense,
This big year, so driven, intense.
There's no reason, no rhyme
For such use of my time,
And no justice in such an expense.

Over Half-done (7/18/08)

The year is over half done.
The race is more than half-run;
The birding's been great,
So, whatever my fate,
It's been cool; it's been neat; it's been fun.

But there's something that now must be said.
It is swirling about in my head.
It is grim to miss birds—
Too depressing for words.
It's a certainty I'm facing with dread.

Already it's just as I feared—
The growing list of birds disappeared.
They've stopped calling or hid.
Is it something I did?
Second-guessing a bird can be weird.

It's much too late to quit now.
It would be just like breaking a vow.
In spite of the cost
And the sleep that I've lost,
I'll keep on, though I can't fathom how.

Big Year Pelagic* (8/23/08)

Like a wobbly yellow duck in a bathtub full of waves,
Our boat is bobbing wildly. I hope my gut behaves.
Yesterday the birds were great. I even added five.
Today is just a rerun. I guess that I'll survive.
Every bird that's added is a bird no longer sought,
Sort of like in fishing when a fish that's caught is caught.
It's funny that the birds now are coming one by one,
Nothing like in winter when the search was just begun.
Will they come out even – the time and birds remaining?
Whatever is the outcome, I'll do without complaining,
And so, I'll keep my travel by boats and planes and cars,
And all the time I'll say my prayers and wish upon the stars.

*There is more about my pelagic adventures in a separate section of this book.

BIRDING TIMES, A LIFE IN RHYMES

Questions (9/12/08)

I waited to see whether poetry could fill up my brain,
Now that I found myself stuck once again on a plane.
I thought of the birds that I'd seen in the months gone before,
And the as-of-yet hidden birds that were lying in store.
My mind traveled back to my innocence in late December—
What had I been thinking? I just couldn't remember.
Did I think that I'd sail through this year and not be demented?
Did I think that this unceasing mania could be prevented?
I think I just launched out and trusted the fates to protect me,
And gave not a thought to the things that might rile or upset me.
Perhaps when it's done and my life is less of a blur,
I will think that what's happened is what was "supposed' to occur.

Mindless (9/25/08)

Mindless mind, brainless brain.
Some things are too hard to explain.
Roads keep winding, never ending,
What's with all this time I'm spending?
But no matter – I keep going,
All the while, not really knowing.
When I get there, will I find it?
If I do not, will I mind it?
Three more months – I've got to do it,
Otherwise, I'll know I blew it.
I tell myself—I must remember:
No more chances past December.

Big Year (10/1/08) (Still flying; now on plane from Denver to Seattle)

B is for Boy; this has been hard to do.
I is for Ignorance, that's part of it too.
G is for Great when a new bird's been found.
Y is for Yelp when the bird's not around
E is for Each of the birds of this year.
A is for All that it's taken; I fear that
R is for Rest that I'll need when it's done.

In spite of that truth: it's really been fun!

Obsession (10/10/08)

Obsession's my name and birding's my game.
It won't be the same when this year is over.
I've had hunting to do, but soon I'll be through.
I expect I'll be blue—no longer a rover.

The effort's been fun, though I've been on the run,
And I've hardly begun to know what I'm doing.
The hopes and the fears, the laughter and tears,
My life in arrears, the fabric ungluing.

Not sorry or grieving, no doubt just believing:
This "thing" needs achieving, and so I'll keep at it.
The end now in sight, not wrong and not right.
It's been a good fight, but still, I say "drat it!"

Florida in Fall (10/23/08)

Eight stilt-legged flamingos
Lined up on the shore.
Could you really ask,
Do I still want more?
Seven Smooth-billed Anis
Peeking from the weeds,
Number 700!
Yet I have more needs.
Multitudes of Mynas
Near the Burger King
Finally, I can count them*
Makes me want to sing.

*The ABA (American Birding Association) rules say that an introduced bird species is not officially countable until after the bird experts say that it has been established in the wild. While I had seen the Common Myna earlier in the year, it only became countable in the middle of the year. The Smooth-billed Ani was species #700 for my ABA big year.

Birding Song (10/23/08)

With all the great composers
Music through them streams,
Instead of counting sheep,
They're singing in their dreams.

What is it with me?
Birding is my song.
Birding makes my life.
Birding all year long.

Chuckling in my sleep,
What a glorious day!
My eyes keep popping open,
There's stuff I've got to say.

Nine-tenths (11/25/08)

The end is so near, but really, it's not,
And where I am now, I would never have thought
That I would now be at seven fourteen
Species that is – an awful lot seen!
But will I stop now? No, of course not, because
When I look back someday at the big year that was,
I don't want to regret not trying to find,
Some possible bird. Of course, losing my mind
Is a real risk as well. Perhaps it's too late
To worry about that. But whatever my fate
I'm exceedingly glad I embarked on this year!
Thirty-six days remain—the end is so near!!

LYNN E. BARBER

A Big Year's End (12/16/08)

I thought it would end with the red, white and blue,*
A grosbeak, a bunting and a lovely swan too,
But swans have big wings and apparently fly,
And the bunting was brown, and exceedingly shy.
The grosbeak was green, not a smidgen of red,
So, when it was all debated and said:
I was clueless, unknowing, blindly running a race,
So, I guess if there's red, it is found in my face.

*Three rarities: Crimson-collared Grosbeak (female is not red); Whooper Swan that I could not find in Idaho; and Blue Bunting (female is brown)

Dread (12/26/08)

Oft during this year I've had low-level dread
That made me just need to curl up in my bed.
The fears of more snow, or road-slippery ice,
Of scary plane rides that were not very nice,
Of rushing wild rivers, and rough tossing seas,
Of crashing my car, or losing my keys,
Of losing a trail, or losing my dream,
And so, when it ends, it surely should seem
That life is more gentle and days have less stress,
Except I will surely still need to address,
My need to go birding, to chase and to find,
And somehow to harness my bird-obsessed mind.

Solitary (12/26/08)

Doing a big year is a solitary quest,
Even if that's not what you like best.
The planning, the reading, the learning, the worry,
The decisions on when to go slow, when to hurry,
The places you go, the places you skip,
The decisions you make on timing each trip.
Though some of the birding is done with your friends,

The success of it all really depends
On being able, alone, to bear your mistakes,
To keep going alone, with whatever it takes,
Through days of no birds, and days when they're found,
To keep keeping on, when there's no one around.

Over (12/28/08)

The big year is over, though three days remain.
I guess I could go out looking again,
But I really can't fathom what I could still find.
There is no possibility that comes to my mind.
There're birds I should have gotten, no doubt.
Still, I'm really quite happy with how it turned out.

Driving to Rockport with Shar, Our Dog (12/31/08)

Hello, I'm mellow-
I just finished a wonderful big year.
And so, I know,
That one thing is unbelievably clear.
It's not, as I thought,
That I'm tired or mourning or sad,
But it's joy, like a buoy:
I'm remembering the joy of the very good time that I had.

Big Year (12/31/08)

B is for Big Year, one of which I've just done.
I is for Incredible and Interesting – and fun!
G is for Going out birding, nonstop,
Obsessive, compulsive and over the top.
Y is for Yes to each chase, to each trip.
E is for Each helpful person and tip.
A is for All of the people I met.
R is for Repaying on mountains of debt.
A Big Year it has been in so many ways:
The Birds, the miles, the fullness of days.

Alaska Big Year (2016)

Gambell

The birding in Gambell, a long ways away,
Is "very unique" as my friend James would say.
Beginning with sea watch 'cross waves to the west,
And then to the boneyards, the part I like best.
You never can tell if a bird will arise,
It might be the usual or a welcome surprise.
A redpoll, a pipit, accentor or lark,
No matter the bird, it's no walk in the park.
We walk or we ride, the road it is rough,
Yet we keep keeping on. We birders are tough.
Yet the birds, they are sparse and hidden from view,
It would have been nice to get one more bird that's new.
Thanks Aaron and James and Bob and the rest,
A WBA* trip – the best of the best.

*Wilderness Birding Adventures (Alaska)

Alaska Wild (6/7/16)

Stark dark mountains, down streaked with snow,
Wild waves crashing on shore,
Geese in the sky, musk ox below,
Adventure and so much more.

Gyrfalcons nesting, high on the rocks,
Snowy Owls sitting on sand,
A quick glimpse of a kinglet, a slow-loping fox
A vast, spectacular land.

Tussocky tundra, moss-covered stones,
Cliffs that are crowded with birds,
Luscious green plants over black earth and bones,
The contrasts much greater than words.

Tall dripping forests, broad treeless plains,
Islands dotting the seas,
High-soaring eagles, loud-calling cranes,
A place never failing to please.

Shorelines of boulders, a flat wave-lapped beach,
Blue skies or rains-clouds above,
Small darting wrens, a bird out of reach,
A state demanding my love.

No Ivory Gulls (11/14/16) During my Alaska big year, Ivory Gulls, needing icebergs, were just too far offshore to be seen.

A few more eiders, a lot more ice,
Some Ivory Gulls would have been quite nice.
A quickie try (just had to try).
I guess I kiss the gull goodbye.

WISCONSIN BIG YEAR (2022) AND MORE

Snowy Owl Search (1/14/22)

Scanning, scanning, scanning
Looking for an owl.
Going out each day
In weather, fair or foul.
Don't know if I'll find one,

Always it's unknown.
Could be where I'm looking,
Or it could have flown.

Bird Seeking (1/31/22)

Twelve degrees. Frosted trees.
Crows, the only birds around.
Feasting eyes, sky-blue skies,
Lots of miles, northward bound.
Sort of knowing, where I'm going,
At the tip-top of the state.
Miles of pine the roads define.
Am I nuts? There's no debate.
Spruce and birches, lots of perches,
Where I'd like a bird to be.
Any bird, how absurd,
Wanting now, just one to see!

Seeking (2/1/22)

Sounds, but not the bird I seek.
The wind is making branches creak.
There seem to be no birds around,
At least not any that I've found.
Then a Raven, dancing, high,
Crosses under lead-gray sky.

Birding (2/26/22)

I'm a person who doesn't love danger or fear.
I don't want to run rapids or jump from a plane.
Chasing a bird is what gives me excitement,
Even when missing the bird brings me pain.

Seeing the bird, however, is priceless.
Seeing a bird, any bird, brings me pleasure.
It brightens my day, enlivens my soul –
Memories of joy and memories to treasure.

Sigh (4/4/22)

It's one of those days when nothing goes as planned,
As if the birds I seek had been completely banned.

Birding (5/3/22)

A million miles I've driven, or so it seems,
Both while awake, or in my dreams.
My eyelids drop. I'm half asleep,
But I have promises to keep.
Birds to seek, to hear, to see.
Birds that must not escape or flee.
Each bird I find, a precious thing
That fills my soul and makes me sing.

Looking Back (8/5/24)

I first experienced what is described below when I was in high school on a biology field trip when this species could be found in central Wisconsin. Now, their range is much more limited in Wisconsin. I made a special trip to Namekagon Barrens Wildlife Area in the northwestern part of the state during my Wisconsin big year, and each of the two years since then so that I could see, and hear, these riveting birds. When I lived in South Dakota, I saw them regularly around the state where they are quite common.

I'm sitting in a blind as morning tints the sky.
As I wait, alone, a silhouette I spy:
Unearthly hoots and cries, the sound of stamping feet.
I sigh in great relief – my trip is now complete.

Strutting Sharp-tailed Grouse, fat with wings outspread,
The racket of each male with purple on his head,
Displaying, racing here, running over there,
Facing off each other in a silent stare.
A springtime mating ritual; as old as prairie land,
A place as full of memories as it is full of sand.

TO CHASE OR NOT TO CHASE

It turns out that even when I'm not doing a big year, the need to chase arises. Sometimes I give in, but often I fight it.

Seeking (7/29/22)

I look and I look and I look,
And then what I look for is found.
Now what should I look for,
When there's nothing, nothing around?

The joy is most in the seeking,
The hunting, the running, the chase.
Somewhat less in the finding.
It's all about the race.

Learning to appreciate the once sought,
When unchased it now is in view:
A challenge, surprisingly elusive,
Making something, now old, into new.

More Thoughts on Chasing (6/9/23)

I've been losing my sleep, every night, every day.
I must chase those birds, or they'll get away.
Can't get to sleep, must get up early.
Making my days all a-haze and a-swirly.
Now that I've let myself get a wink,
The answer is much more clear than I think:
Lie down in the shade, close my eyes, take a nap.
Ignore the bird songs – they are surely a trap.

Chasing (11/17/23)

So, what do you do when you give up bird chasing,
The frenzy and panic, the time always racing?
You sit down to write, and you hope that the writing
Will bring the same joy, will be so exciting
That instead of bird hunting and seeking and fretting,
You'll now hunt for words, but still not forgetting
The wonder, the joy, the great birding days,
The pleasures birds bring in so many ways.

Sigh – No Longer Doing Big Years (12/12/23)

I must admit – I miss the thrill.
I want to go and climb that hill.
A little rosy-finch is waiting,
But I am not participating.

Birding To Bird (3/20/24)

Birding to bird – what an odd thought.
See what you see, not what you ought.
If I find a rare bird, that would be fine,
But nowadays, that's not by design.

Not Chasing (4/8/24)

I hear of a rare bird, but I don't want to chase.
I don't want to run; I don't want to race.
I want to go slowly, to hear and to look.
I want to find out if what they say in the book
Is true of this bird. Or is it unique?
I want to be finding. I don't want to seek.
I want to discover, be surprised and be learning.
I want, if I can, from the chase to be turning.

Okay (6/27/24)

I've been doing big years for nearly 20 years.
But maybe I'm over it. Maybe? Perhaps.
Then – I hear of a rarity sighting,
And my resolutions, my abstinence, threaten collapse.

My head says, "Let's quit. Stop! That's enough!"
But my heart and my gut want to go, want to chase.
What is my problem? What should I do?
This is a pattern that I need to erase.

Okay. Settle down. I still can go birding.
I can stop, breathe in deeply, and I can let go.
The birding will clearly be just as rewarding,
When birds are seen and heard – going slow.

For example, just now an oriole is singing.
A Warbling Vireo is high in the trees.
Somewhere there's a pewee slowly saying his name.
This is the type of day I should seize.

A Chipping Sparrow preens. A Swamp Sparrow trills.
And all around me are trees of green.
Slowly a Red-eyed Vireo is talking
Though muted and gentle, my enjoyment is keen.

Just (7/16/24)

I just want to go birding.
I want to stop chasing.
But what new obsession
Is chasing replacing?

Is it music? Is it painting?
Is it sleeping? Is it writing?
What fills my soul and
Is fun and exciting?

Maybe a balance.
Now there's an odd thought.
A bit of moderation?
(or maybe not).

A Resolution. Again. (7/24/24)

As an exalted bird chaser of the highest degree,
I feel I must explain what this all means to me.

When it's January first, and a year is beginning,
A new list begins – a year for the winning.

It's a brand-new big year – every day, always racing.
Over here! Now it's there! Place to place. Always chasing.

Another kind of chase, though intense, less inspiring
Is adding life-birds, done in spurts, and less tiring.

As I think of past chases, all the joy, all the wonder,
In the depths and the heights, the calm and the thunder,

Though I'm so very glad for each bird, for each sighting,
It's time, now, I think, for a little less fighting.

A little less stressing about birds, and the weather,
A little less effort how to put it together.

Now I guess I'm a dabbler, carefully choosing my chases,
Choosing when I will bird, which birds, and which places.

Though inside I still yearn, wanting and needing,
With my age, birding urges are finally receding.

Yet each time I hear of a bird that's discovered,
My heart leaps inside – hidden obsession, uncovered.

Should I leap from my chair, resolutions displacing?
Probably not, usually not. I'll refrain from new chasing.

Yes or No (8/23/24)

Some years are birdy. Others not so much.
I've drifted away. I admit – I've lost touch.

HUMMINGBIRDS

Rufous Hummingbird (Rufie)* (4/4/09, I think)

I want to tell you, little hummer:
You turned my winter into summer.
To have you drink my preparation,
Gave me cause for celebration.
Your "tick-tick" welcome, your levitating,
I found especially exhilarating.
And when you hovered in mid-air
And snapped at gnats that were not there,
I knew that cuteness was your name,
And I would never be the same.
I know of course you'll soon be leaving,
And I, as surely, will be grieving.
Yet joy I have, and deep thanksgiving,
Your presence gives such joy to living.

*A female Rufous Hummingbird came to our Fort Worth feeders for nine consecutive winters, sometimes staying from August to April; we called her "Rufie," but Rufie may have been more than one bird, for nine years is a long time for a hummingbird to live.

Rufie Lament (8/10/10)

It's happened again; it happens most years –
A hummingbird leaves, and I'm left in tears.
A smidgen of energy, rufous-tinged glow,
I knew when she came that she also would go.
Each time she arrived, flitting here, flitting there,
Came sweetness and sorrow I hardly could bear,
A capsule of life, what we all must go through,
We are here, we are gone, and that's why I'm blue.

Humm (to the tune of "I've Grown Accustomed to Her Face" from *My Fair Lady*) (10/22/20)

I've grown accustomed now to Humm. She almost makes the day begin,
She's extremely independent, but she also needs my aid.
She really should be somewhere else, but instead she's stayed.
I've grown accustomed now to Humm.

I've grown accustomed now to Humm. I take her feeders out each morn.
If only I could keep her warm and safe in every way,
Worries would be lessened; I'd have nothing more to say.
I've grown accustomed now to Humm.

I've grown accustomed now to Humm. She always makes the days fly by.
Every time she flies away, I wonder if she's left.
I know that I should feel relief. Instead, I feel bereft.
I've grown accustomed now to Humm.

I've grown accustomed now to Humm. She's a tiny spark of life.
There is something that enlivens me, with every sip she takes,
Bringing joy into a world that even sun forsakes.
I've grown accustomed now to Humm.

"Humm" is the name I gave the female Anna's Hummingbird that at the time of this writing, October 22, 2020, had been seen for 57 days in our Anchorage yard.

Prose about Humm…(10/30/20)

Every morning now, when it is still very dark, I take up my position at the kitchen sink, peering out the kitchen window into the black backyard toward the still invisible hummingbird feeders. Then I peer out at the birch tree where the Anna's Hummingbird has recently begun to periodically perch as well as at her previous usual perch tree. And I wait and watch. About 30 minutes before official dawn this morning when I was finally able to see a few things with my binoculars, I saw a dark spot fuzzily silhouetted against the birch trunk. Wonder of wonders the spot began to move and then flew to her favorite feeder. She had survived another cold night, this one at 18 degrees! And, as has begun to be usual, I immediately burst into tears of relief and joy. Another day with Humm had begun. Day 65.

(11/1/20) I have made this feeding of the Anna's Hummingbird into nearly a full-time job. No pay except the possibly (probably?) temporary reward of seeing her return to the feeders each morning before dawn and throughout each day. The temperature stayed near a windy zero degrees much of this morning, and even when it rose to about 20, it felt like zero. I have a generally flat feeder out in the yard that she seems to prefer. Because it needs to be brought in to thaw every hour or so, I finally found a similar, though larger feeder that I can use to exchange with it, and she readily now feeds from whichever feeder is out there and I don't have to have an empty feeder space in the yard during thawing. So, that problem is solved.

On the back porch I have two other feeders that she also goes to, a heated upright feeder and another upright feeder which has become my nutrient feeder. The heated feeder has difficulty keeping the water from freezing at these temperatures, but it works best with a reduced volume of sugar water, so the little light bulb only has a small amount of water that it needs to keep it from freezing. Today I've thawed and reduced the water in it twice and maybe it's staying thawed for now. That is particularly important if I forget to exchange warmed feeders with the other frozen ones.

The feeder that I use to add organic nutrients to her diet (no evident insects are around that would usually serve that purpose) is another one that she seemed to prefer in the warmer weather with plain sugar water in it. Unfortunately, when she came to the nutrient mix the first time I offered it to her a few days ago, which I had prepared according to the package, she ate only briefly and clearly did not like it and did not return to what had earlier been a favorite eating spot (the nutrient mix colors the water yellow and has an odor). So, the next day I made it more dilute, figuring that if she ate any nutrients at all, it would be better than none. But again, she sampled it and did not like it apparently. So yesterday, I made it up at a more reduced concentration and also dissolved the mixture in sugar water instead of the plain water the directions stated to use (the nutrient mix has sugars as well as vitamins and amino acids). She ate it repeatedly! And she ate it again today (I make it new each day because that is what the label says). When it is thawing, I briefly put out plain sugar water in another feeder. As I was writing this she came briefly for some nutrients, actually landing on the porch railing for a while. Life is good. Sadly, we have many months to go of weather this cold and colder. If all goes very well, I will have no vacation for weeks and weeks and weeks. I can only hope.

Anna's Hummingbird and Anchorage Snow (late October 2020)

I peer intently – I just can't see.
Vague shapes appear where trees should be.
A world of white – it just was brown.
And still it falls, keeps falling down.
She's here! I see her now against the snow.
Oops! She's gone. Where did she go?
She'll come more often as daylight comes,
The little bird of winging hums.
The jays now come with squawks and calls.
Magpies too. And still it falls.
Six more months? I guess it's so.
The snow will stay, but she will go.

Humm Again (11/5/20)

I'll cry if I see her today; I'll cry if she doesn't come.
The continuing? Over? Amazing! Remarkable saga of Humm.
She arrived so late yesterday. It was startling to see her at all,
In temperatures way below naught, this little bundle of small.
Feathers all fluffed up, she'd sit, would drink and then disappear,
A wonderful part to my life; her dying is what I now fear.
Or maybe miracles are, and she's just in a torporous state.
It's likely I'll never know what happened, or ever learn her fate.
Ho Humm! I heave a sigh.
I'm afraid it's time to say good-by.
That tiny bird filled every day.
She was my work; she was my play.

Missing Humm (to tune of "I Don't Know How to Love Him") (11/5/20)

I don't know how to care for her, what to do,
    how to feed her.
She is small, yes really small.
In these past few months, she's been all my world,
    I've given her my all.
I don't know how to take this,

>　　　how to fill all my empty days,
She's a bird, she's just a bird,
And I've seen so many birds before,
>　　　in very many ways, she's just one more.
How to give her warmth, how to keep her well, Did I do enough? Only time will tell
I never thought I'd come to this, for a hummingbird.
Don't you think it's rather funny
>　　　that I should be in this position?
I'm the one who counts the birds,
>　　　yet now I cry, and wonder why
Why she had to go,
>　　　I miss her so.

Hummingbirds (6/24/24)

When I see a hummer, it makes me smile,
Though I've seen them often, or it's been a while.

LYNN E. BARBER

OTHER TIMES, MORE LIFE, MORE RHYMES

Volunteering (Non-church and Non-bird Related)

Over the years I have been involved in many different nonprofit groups in addition to churches, as a general member and as a board member or officer. The ones with which I spent the most time are the ACLU (city and state-wide groups in North Carolina), the United Nations Association in NC, the North Carolina Human Rights Coalition, the Poor People's Campaign in Alaska, and many, many bird-related groups including Wake Audubon (NC), the Carolina Bird Club, Fort Worth Audubon, the Texas Ornithological Society, Northern Hills Bird Club (SD), South Dakota Ornithologists Union, Anchorage Audubon Society, Wausau Bird Club (WI) and the Wisconsin Society for Ornithology . Sometimes I even wrote poems about them, generally while I was stuck in a meeting room.

ACLU Awards Banquet (2/1/97)

All around me liberals sit,
At ease we are among our friends.
The yearly CLU awards,
The long-fought fight that never ends.

Awards for courage, honor, work,
A time for sharing and applause,
Holding up the Bill of Rights,
And those who've given to the Cause.

We need these times to give us strength,
To lift us up, to help us cope,
To charge our spirits, send us forth,
To inspire us all and give us hope.

United Nations Association Convention (6/6/97)

A group of people gathered. In Washington, D.C.
Those of great experience, beginners, including me.

Debating resolutions, hearing issues aired.
Feeling hope arise, where often I've despaired.

I thank the UNA, and those who make it strong.
It's clear this is a group where each of us belong.

We each have our agendas, our axes, so to speak,
Our backgrounds and our viewpoints – each of us, unique.

Of course, we don't agree on everything proposed,
Arguments, impassioned pleas, in favor and opposed.

Yet there is overarching, a deep sincere concern,
That peace and justice flourish, that everyone should learn,

That waging war leads nowhere, that wisdom leads to peace,
That we must work unceasing, that war itself might cease.

And so, we sit and ponder, negotiate, learn skills,
And lobby our officials to pay the UN bills.

At a Local UNA Meeting in Black Mountain, NC (7/26/97)

I see people here, tired and spent,
Their lives have been given. Who knows where they went?

Uncounted hours, stories not told.
I have done nothing, yet I'm in the fold.

How can I hear them, learn what they've done,
Weep for their failures, sing where they've won?

How can I learn, and continue the fight,
Build on their building, bring day out of night?

Do they feel hopeless? Do they feel grief?
Or do they just exhale with a sigh of relief,

That others must carry the burden they've borne,
As each of us works for a free, peaceful morn.

Although they have worked, and I've not begun,
We still work together on the job to be done.

At Another Meeting (4/25/98)

It seems that my life is full of long meetings.
Mostly I sit in a variety of seatings.

Dim dingy rooms without decoration,
Or golfing resorts (without a vacation).

Lengthy reports, many glazed eyes.
Times of debate and heated replies.

Weighty discussions with substantial import,
Laughing and joking and other such sport.

Where would I be if not at this spot?
At some other meeting, as likely as not.

At a UNA Meeting in Washington, D.C. (6/3/98)

A feeling of hopelessness; the same old lament:
The money the U.S. ought to have spent.

Where will it end? Will the UN kick us out:
It seems nearly certain, without any doubt.

In our annual assault on Congress's halls,
Continually ramming our heads into walls,

The bane of our lives, the demon, unfazed,
Is Jesse, our own, our Senator, crazed.

Dead-set against peace, against justice and rights,
Ignoring the issue, promoting the fights.

Invincible, immortal, an unending foe,
His homey unwaveringness always our woe.

"Patience," we say through each 6-year term,
"It's got to get better," -- the turn of the worm?

And still he goes on. Will his reign never end?
Will our UN survive 'til we turn 'round the bend"

Somehow our message is not being heard.
We cannot give up now! We shall not be deterred!

On Facing the Opposition – Political or Otherwise (6/4/98)

The inherent frustration when opponents collide,
And factions within factions, the right and left side,

No matter the issue, how big or how small,
There are bitter hard-liners, who won't listen at all.

A benign resolution seems so hard to find,
When everyone's patience is left far behind.

We each think the truth (and God) is with us,
And we can't understand why there's such a big fuss.

We know the way that things *should* occur.

The others are ignorant, misguided, unsure.

The disputants keep talking but their ears are closed tight,
Compromise is unthought of. Prepare for a fight!

It's easy to give up, to throw up our hands,
To stop all the striving, abandon our stands,

Walk off the field, concede there's no way.
If we can't win the game, we don't want to play.

We need to keep on, we need to proceed,
In view of how critical, how dire, the need.

Reports on Lobbying (6/5/98)

We're hearing reports of yesterday's chats
With aides for the good guys (and also, the rats).

A small bit of hope, a bit of despair,
Lament for the ignorance we found everywhere.

Unfortunately, many delegates feel the need to orate,
To hold forth at length on the state of the State.

Needing to Cut Back (6/5/98) (Periodically, when the stress of over-involvement in activities and work got to me, I made the necessary decision to say "no", always hard for me.)

They're good people all, well-meaning, sincere,
But my heart is not here, or anywhere near.

A muffle of voice, laughter, a speech,
There's much I could learn, and much they could teach.

Yet my life is so full, so much I would do.
I cannot do everything – perhaps one or two.

It's as if I had died and looked down from on high,
Had gently departed without a good-by.
A slow realization of a limited me:
I cannot be everything I wish I could be.

I belong in our church and in all that they do.
I belong with the birders, conservation, too.

It's there that I feel I have something to give.
It's there that I know there's life left to live.

The rest, though enticing, is not where I'm at.
There are others whose lives are devoted to that.

It means letting go, cutting back, saying no,
Setting priorities wherever I go.

At a Multicultural Meeting (3/7/99)

Nobody knows the trouble we'll cause.
Where on earth are we going?
How can we turn our words into deeds?
Where is the energy flowing?

All is so general, vague and obscure.
Minds in the clouds, future unclear.
The ground is not stable, the footing is shaky.
The future is scary. We face it with fear.

This is *my* goal. Yours seems to differ.
Are we working together? Are we aimed the same way?
I hope that we are, that the progress will come,
That we'll all stay the course and not go astray.

Problem (probably July, 1999) Every now and then a person comes along who creates great waves of disaster around him/her; this poem relates the real story of one such person and was written before we knew how it would all turn out as is clear from the options in the second-to-last verse.

There once was a woman named ___,
Who washed in like flotsam and jetsam.
She was nobody's fool.
When she smiled and was cruel
As she gloated, "I got 'em, I got some"

As she worried the people around her
There was nothing that seemed to confound her,
Though bland and all smiles,
She was using her wiles,
And nothing could ever astound her.

She actually was often quite charming,
Which in retrospect seems quite alarming.
We'd think, "She's with us,
What was all the fuss?"
She'd delude us and be so disarming.

From the very first day, she has failed us,
As first anger and then doubt assailed us.
She has shaken our boat,
Had a hold of our throat,
And she really has nearly derailed us.

Who she is, we did not understand,
Or that things could get so out hand,
What we thought was her love
Was a fist in a glove,
Not anything like we had planned.

I cannot really portray it.
I can't even begin to convey it.
The grief she has brought,
The harm she has wrought,
Nearly no one would ever nay-say it.

We never thought we would outlast her,
The demon disguised as a pastor,
Dissension and grief
Without any relief,
A depressing deadly disaster.

So, at last it came to the meeting,
With almost not quite enough seating.
With her forces arrayed
And not even dismayed,

    a) We all got a terrible beating.
    b) Her ego at last her defeating.

And so is the end of my story,
Through a hell that was bloody and gory
She has routed our troops,
Split us in groups,
Of course, she believes, to her glory.

In Raleigh at a Poor People's Campaign Gathering/Workshop
(2/8/18)

We yearn, we listen. What can we do?
How will the beauty of all come through?

How will the poor have life that's just?
We must take action, oh yes, we must!

Each one of us is only one.
But there's a job to do that must be done!

What we will do – the path's unclear –
All I know is, I'm glad I'm here!

CHURCHY STUFF

Even as a fanatic birder, I must admit that not everything that is important is about birds. For all my life I have been involved in churches in one way or another, as a child in Sunday School, in college in various discussion groups and as a publicity chair and newsletter editor, as a member, officer and moderator of a few UCC (United Church of Christ) churches in the cities where we lived, and as a pastor's wife. My concept of God and religion is a constantly changing thing, but often it is present in my thoughts and becomes part of my poems. Over the years I have been involved in various groups reading and studying the Bible. Often when we were asked to take some time to jot down our thoughts, my thoughts turned to rhyme, trying to put the meanings I was finding into verse. I have only included a sampling of my Bible verse poems here. Even though for most of my life I have not mixed my birding writing and my other writing, a book about my life would not be complete without at least a sampling of my rhymes in which religion/God/church play a part. But first...

A Quick Question to You, the Reader of this book about "Churchy" Rhymes (12/15/21)

Does my mention of things such as God and faith
Make you want to run and flee far away?
Please wait! I really have no intention
Of trying to make you convert or pray.
It's just that these things are part of me
And have crept in or pushed their way into rhyme.
Of course, you can skip them and read other poems,
Or read these. It really won't take very much of your time.

We Are Supposed to Identify Our Gifts (10/12/97)

For many years we were involved as participants and then leaders in a group (CLAY; Faith-to-Focus) involved in helping people discern their gifts and who they are and what their ministry might be; it was this group that was instrumental in both Dave and I changing careers mid-life.

Identifying gifts – I'm a leader on the team.
It's one of my gifts, I surmise.
Gifts are found where you'd never believe.
It should no longer come as surprise.

Some of my gifts I don't want and don't claim.
Others I celebrate and embrace.
And then there are gifts that I wish that I had,
And others that seem out of place.

But I'm me, so it seems, the good and bad,
The useful, the not ever used,
The potential for things I've not ever dreamed,
The need to become unconfused.

Each time I attempt to discern a clear path,
A couple more steps come into view.
It certainly is worth all the effort and time.
And maybe someday I'll know what to do.

Gifts (10/12/97)

Listing gifts, big and small.
Am I finished? Is that all?
Laughter, joy and time to give,
Love of future; urge to live.
Rhythms, music, fill my soul,
Where there's music, I am whole.

Meeting deadlines, pleasing clients,
Generally, without defiance.
Energy, undimmed belief
That I can do it, without grief,
Fill my time with many things.
When it's right, my heart still sings.

Discussion of Mark 10:35-45 (10/15/97)

James and John wanted top billing.
They told Jesus to grant it, but he didn't agree.
"You don't know what you're asking," he said disapproving.
"It's God who decides it; it's really not me."

The disciples were clearly unhappy
At the nerve of the two, who thought they were best.
Then Jesus stepped in, said you must be a servant;
Your humbleness quotient must meet the test.

The point of it all is to seek to serve others,
Not to claw your way to the top.
If everyone's goal is to help those who need it,
The bickering for glory will come to a stop.

    Note: we read these Bible verses and then were asked to think and write our thoughts. As usual, mine came out in rhyme.

Quick Rhyming Thoughts (10/26/97)

A few minutes to squeeze in a poem.
I'm filled to the brim with thoughts I could rhyme.
Which will I choose for this brief time I have?
Probably none. I won't have the time.

What energizes me is making you smile,
Easing your burdens, lightening your day,
Meeting your glance, connecting our hearts.
It fills my heart to give joy away.

Another Church Activity (10/26/97)

"Look and listen" is the core activity,
What it means is seeking indicators of call,
Areas of passion to which we respond,
Areas to which we could give our all.

I don't know what it means that I have many passions,
It means that I'm spread astoundingly thin,
How to refine it and narrow the focus.
I'm still seeking just how to begin.

I could chuck it all out and begin it all over,
Erase the slate so to speak and rethink
Just what I should do with all of my energy,
Or is there some way that they all interlink?

Part of the problem is that all of my life
I've done everything with haste without pause,
When the essence of life doesn't come easy
Suddenly the world is lacking in laws.

Retreat Thoughts (11/8/97)

It's the Faith-to-Focus retreat.
Everyone's quiet, lost deep in thought,
Discerning, divining where we are going,
Seeking again, what we often have sought.

This is not something that is easy to do.
How do we know what we feel is a call?
Are we seeking for something glorious and grand?
Is it that wee little voice? Is that really all?

And if it's that voice, what is it saying?
Is it English or French or a language unknown?
It seems to get quiet whenever I listen.
It's changing directions, or maybe it's flown.

But I know it is there, there isn't a doubt.
I know there is value in staying the course.
The search itself is a treasure to me,
And I'm pulled ever on by a life-giving force.

Last Session (11/16/97)

It's the scary time now -- making a plan.
What to do next, as if anyone knows.
It's nearly unanimous, the scratching of heads.
What does it mean? What do you suppose?

Now to get personal and look at myself,
I've made no real progress, it now seems to me.
I still feel a pull, or rather a few.
But the direction of pull – what can it be?

I need to create, be it little or small.
I do feel fulfillment in work with my hands.
But I also am driven toward more time with birds,
Especially birding in far distant lands.

If there was a way to work for a living,
Creating and birding all wrapped into one,
I think I'd have made it, have reached heaven's gate.
But would it be "ministry", or only just fun.

It seems so self-serving, doing what I like,
Arranging my life to fit my own needs.
Where is the outreach, the helping, the good?
I need to feel good by doing good deeds.

Yet helping others to see into nature,
Helping them treasure a part of creation,
That could be a good deed that I do for them.
I guess that I'm needing a re-evaluation.

Trying to Be Part of a Community (3/8/98)

We gather at church, a community, true,
But often divisions split us in two.

Strong faithful people doing our best,
Yet sometimes our doing puts faith to the test.

Compassion and caring are sometimes ignored,
In our daily endeavor of serving the Lord.

Praising (5/6/98)

Praising God – I'm big on praising.
Somehow it resonates within.
Unlike praying or asking mercy,
So much easier to begin.

Envision singing, dancing, leaping,
Lifting soul and heart in praise,
Turning frowns to smiles of gladness,
Thanking God in many ways.

If everyone would work on praising,
Anger, selfishness would wane.
Life would lose a bit of sorrow.
Grace would live amidst the pain.

In the Beginning (7/25/98)

In the beginning was the Word, unnoticed and unheard,
And then came the creation, and the singing of a bird.

From a timeless void of dark, unformed, chaotic, stark,
Came the cooing of the dove, and the melody of lark.

From a universal hush, came the organ of the thrush.
Avian music awoke the earth in one tumultuous rush.

Bible Botany and Zoology (12/2/98) (support group at church - Is. 11:1-10; Ps. 72:1-7,8-19; Rom. 15:4-13; Matt. 3:1-12)

A bit of botany in the Bible today:
A shoot from a stump, from roots comes a bough.
The pharisees and Sadducees need to bear fruit;
God is like rain that falls on grass now.

And then come the fauna: the cow and the bear,
The asp and the adder – don't fear to go there.
The calf and the lion, and kids of both kinds:
Biblical lessons for biological minds.

Without (4/4/99)

Who am I with no one here?
Apart from people, places, things.
Do I exist, apart from them?
A slight discomfort this thought brings.

If I should fall, with no one near,
Would I be falling or a dream?
Is who I am "reality"?
Are life and living what they seem?

A butterfly that stirs the air
Can ripple through eternity.
If I had never walked the earth,
What would earth lack, if lacking me?

An integral, though tiny part
Of God's creation, not yet done,
While hope and health may wane or flee,
God's work through me has just begun.

Praise (unknown date)

The sun will shine, the fog will lift.
What will it be, God's newest gift?

I cannot tell, I cannot guess.
All I can say is "Amen, oh yes!"
All praise to God with every breath,
God with us from our birth to death.
I will open my heart; I will sing with my voice.
I will give praise and will shout "Rejoice!"

Awaiting God (12/11/04) (Advent 2004)

God is still speaking – that sign is so clear.
But what is God saying? And what will I hear?
Will the words wrap me gently, and hold me with love,
Or will they pierce through me, like swords from above?
In a world of distractions, loud noises and hurry,
Will the words calm my soul, or fill me with worry?
And what if the speaking is not words at all,
But gestures and sunsets and moments that call?
Somehow my senses – God-given – to me,
Must open and wait for whatever will be.

What Charles Has Wrought (tune: "Camelot") (sometime in 2005 or 2006) This is a tribute to Charles Brown as leader of Life's Journey, sung by what was left of Life's Journey, a singing group founded and led by him.

Said: It's true! It's true! Sir Charles has made it clear.
The music can be zesty all the year.

Our Charles arrived a little while ago here.
We learned that music needed to be hot.
And there's no legal limit to the tunes here.
What Charlies has wrought!

His singing and his playing I'll remember,
And how he memorizes on the spot.
I'm not sure how we'll do it in September,
When Charles is not.

Charles has wrought! Charles has wrought!

I know it sounds a bit bizarre,
But what Charles has wrought—
Our music's come so far.
The music comes together with his styling,
By ten, we're playing without pause or fear.

In short, there's simply not,
A more inspiring spot
Than playing with Life's Journey with
Our Charles, and what he's wrought!
Charles has wrought! Charles has wrought!

I know it gives a person pause,
But what Charles has wrought, Charles has wrought,
In spite of all our flaws,
He helps us blend our music to a group sound,
By 10 am, we're one, no longer five.

In short, there's simply not,
A more inspiring spot,
Than playing with Life's Journey with
Our Charles, and what he's wrought!

Shall We Act? (tune: "Shall We Dance") (sometime in 2005 or 2006) Charles Brown also started a play-reading group where we wrote and then read our creations in church, an experience new and fun for us. Then he dismayed us by getting a preaching job and leaving. I learned when writing this book that Charles died in July, 2024 at the age of 86.

Shall we act? Shall we wear our black garments? Shall we act?
Shall we act? Shall we then let Charles go and pack it in?
Or perchance, we'll continue what we're doing and go on.
Though we're really rank beginners, and we're clueless what we're doing, shall we act, shall we act? WE SHALL ACT, WE SHALL ACT!

Shall we act, shall we follow Charles' directions, shall we act?
Shall we act with abandon though we're really not real actors? Shall we act? WE SHALL ACT, we shall act!

God Is (9/07)

God is in the green things. God is in the sun.
God is in my endings and when I've just begun.
God is in the magic. God's in the mundane.
God's in what seems awful, depressing and insane.
God is where the road just ends and fades away.
God is in the night and continues through the day.
God is in the smiles, the rejoicing and the love.
God is here on earth and also up above.
God is there when we're needing, and in our helping hands.
God's right here beside me and off in foreign lands.
God is in our music, in our singing, in our words.
God is in the critters, especially in birds.
God's where it is raining, where it's cold and where it's hot.
In fact, the more I think on it – there's nowhere God is not!

ONE MUST WORK

For some reason, I rarely wrote poems about my work life – the bacteriology laboratories (1974-1982) or the law office world (1985-2020). Maybe when I wasn't working, I didn't want to think about it. I apparently did write a few poems to be sung at a microbiology Christmas party in late 1980.

Microbiology Lab

Jolly Old St. Nicholas (lab version) (80-81)

Jolly old St. Nicholas, lend your ear this way,
Don't you tell a single soul, what I'm going to say,
Christmas Eve is coming soon, now you dear old man,
Tell me what you'll bring to me, tell me if you can.
Bobby wants a tissue culture, Paul wants a gene,
Lynnie wants a soybean plant, brown and pink and green,

Walt wants cyclic AMP, and Thoyd wants mutants too,
The Gerries want so many things, I don't know what you'll do.
When the clock is striking twelve, when I'm fast asleep,
Down the chimney broad and black, with your pack you'll creep;
All the stockings you will find hanging in a row,
Mine will be shortest one, you'll be sure to know.

Workin' in a Microbio Lab (tune: "Walking in a Winter Wonderland") (80-81)

Timers ring, are ya listenin.?
In the lab, gels are glistening'
I'm hoping tonight, something will go right,
Workin' in a microbio lab.

In the lab, O, we can build a microbe.
Then pretend that it is recombined.
We'll say, "Are you dangerous?" It'll say, "No, man,
But you'd better keep me very well contained."

Later on, we'll perspire
As we streak plates, by the fire,
We'll face unafraid, the chaos that we made,
Workin' in a microbio lab.

Lab Christmas (tune: "Chestnuts Roasting on an Open Fire") (80-81)

Test tubes cooking in an autoclave,
Toxic fumes nipping at your nose,
Research props strewn all over the bench,
And students dressed up in labby clothes.
Everybody knows, a culture that's contaminated,
Helps to make a lousy night.
Tiny vials filled with fuzzy green mold,
Are not a very pretty sight.
For sure, the boss is on the way,
And there are lots of data needed every day,

And every graduate student is gonna try,
To see if microbes really know how to fly,
And so, I'm offering this simple phrase,
To students from one to ninety-two,
Although it's been said, many times, many ways,
My condolences to you.

Thirteen Days of Christmas (1980-81)

On the first day of Christmas, my true love sent to me, a grant for my laboratory.

2. two lyophilizers
3. three microscopes
4. graduate students
5. platinum loops
6. stirrers stirring
7. pipettes draining
8. flasks a-shaking
9. cultures growing
10. gels a-soaking
11. cells a-swimming
12. roaches running

On the thirteenth day of Christmas, Reagan cut the budget, the end of my laboratory.

Law

1985 – Day by Day – a Chronological Poem. I don't remember whether this poem had more verses. Most likely I got too busy, or too bored with the writing, to continue it.

Jan. 1 Tues.- Playing the banjo for hours without end.
Jan. 2 Wed.-Gazing for seconds, into eyes of a friend.
Jan. 3 Thurs. -Learning that clothes are too big, with elation.
Jan. 4 Fri.-Walking downtown with my Bar application.
Jan. 5. Sat.-Shopping and listening and talking with Dad.
Jan. 6. Sun.-Dancing and singing to make my heart glad.
Jan. 7 Mon.-Beginning the last of my law school semesters.

Jan. 8 Tues.-Learning of mortgages, notes, and investors.
Jan. 9 Wed.-Researching on client-to-client communication.
Jan. 10 Thurs.-Staying at home for a snow-day vacation.
Jan. 11 Fri.-Dancing the dances of lands far and near.
Jan. 12 Sat.-Shoveling coal – the one time each year.
Jan. 13 Sun.-Talking on coolies and researching resale.
Jan. 14 Mon.-Reading real estate finance in increasing detail.
Jan. 15 Tues.-Networking with friends and being part of a whole.
Jan. 16 Wed.-Being part of a Council not under control.
Jan. 17 Thurs.-Feeling burdened with tax as a fumbling beginner.
Jan. 18 Fri.-Filing a brief, then a faculty club dinner.
Jan. 19 Sat.-Celebrating our first date; eighteen years ago.
Jan. 20 Sun.-Coming home from church in the ice and the snow.
Jan. 21 Mon.-Staying at home in a world full of ice.
Jan. 22 Tues.-Returning to school, not nearly as nice.
Jan. 23 Wed.-Singing and getting myself to relax.
Jan. 24 Thurs.-Struggling again with corporate tax.
Jan. 25 Fri.-Skipping and twirling and stepping and leaping.
Jan. 26 Sat.-Playing the dulcimer into the time meant for sleeping.
Jan. 27 Sun.-Judging moot court – a most disciplined fight....

Decisions about My Law Career (2/28/85) This was written during my last semester of law school at Duke University, and I was clearly stressed about it.

Wondering and waiting for day after day.
There's an urgency piercing the mist.
There are things I can't speak or write down or display;
A continuous plague with no cease or desist.

I don't even know how I want things to end.
For each argument con, there are arguments pro.
My mind's in a turmoil; despair may descend,
Or elation will come, or I'll drift to and fro.

The future's exciting. There is much that is good.
Yet my soul longs for change as of yet undefined.
I know change will come, and I know that it should,
But it isn't the kind that I once had in mind.

There are moments my body seems scarce to contain
The emotions and dreams, the frustrations and fears.
I'm learning to wait, yet the worries remain,
While [unfinished]...disappears.

A Rare Unrhyming Sort of Poem (3/16/85)

A strange sad, tired anticipation, yearning.
A clear mid-life crisis looms on the horizon.
My mid-life career change precipitating – not being caused by – a mid-life crisis.
Feeling, almost, too old. Too old for any more big changes.
Too old to experience things I never wanted until I realized I might be getting too old to experience them.
Feeling at the peak of being me, of being all that I'll ever be able to be, but shortly to be less.
Feeling the need to be close to people, before I'm not interesting or caring or useful.
The tears are being held in by willpower. The muscles in my throat ache in sadness.

Career Woes (probably mid-1985) I just could not figure out what path forward was the best – continuing at the law firm ("WEDPA") where I had worked during law school, or something else, something more "noble."

She sat in the library, the fluorescent lights humming,
Surrounded by books, with indices, numbing.

She thought of the summer, the turmoil within,
Her hopes for the future, the career to begin.

Had she fallen away from her dreams, from her goal?
Had she bought corporate hype, and sold her own soul?

The questions kept coming, with no answers, no rest.
What was good? Possible? Alternative? Best?

That she might not be offered the job was her fear.
Her heart was on WEDPA, but her head was unclear.

She envisioned herself in a suit, but the thought
Made her wonder and worry – what had law school wrought?

Her earlier visions of aiding the poor
Were deliberately shelved or had flown out the door.

And so, she continued both weary and sad,
To hope and to pray for that which was bad.

10 Years Later - Starting A Solo Law Practice (5/28/96)

Birding, relaxing, enjoyable things,
Blessing my spirit, giving me wings.
But stomach still knots with worry and frets,
The clients I'm getting, the fear of forgets.
The whole thing's too new, the pattern obscure.
Not knowing what's happening; of most things unsure.
The future's uncertain, the pathway unseen
One foot in the past; I'm stuck in between.

Being a Solo Practitioner (6/24/96)

My life is divided into niches and slots,
Some I like less; some I like lots.
The law part at home, fits in better with life,
Allows time for other things, like being a wife.
My conscience controls, or should be, in charge,
To determine vacation, whether smaller or large.
An adult I must be, responsible, wise,

In determining when to do things I despise,
Determining whether I can take a small break,
Guiding each task, each decision I make.

Being Self-employed (7/17/96)

The fact that how I spend my hours
Is mostly mine to choose,
The days go by erratically at speeds that I control.
And when I choose to work, I earn, and when I don't, I lose.

There's no one else in charge of me,
No one to watch or care.
Though that sounds bad, might be I guess,
That's neither here nor there.

The best thing is, I am alone,
With no one I must please.
There's time to work and time to eat
And time to spend 'mong trees.

A whole day here, a weekend there,
A couple weeks I pray.
Time to relax, to bird, of course,
To work hard and to play.

I work at home, the dogs are near,
The setting gives me bliss.
I enjoy the work, in fact would say:
"They're paying me for this?"

Pros and Cons of My Solo Law Practice (7/22/97)

Being restless and lazy and unwilling to work,
I decided that within me a poem might lurk.
About working itself, and my thoughts about how
I view my practice and what I do now.
It's rather complex; it ebbs and it flows.

Although lots of cons, there are many more pros.
On days when energy and ambition wane,
When nothing inspires and fog fills my brain,
It's then I might better be back in a firm,
Or even in science, pursuing a germ.
But mostly, the freedom of working alone,
Doing **my** bills and answering **my** phone,
Excites me, empowers me, fills me with life;
I'm out of the turmoil, dissension and strife.
To know that there's no one who must say okay,
Inspect what I do, control what I say,
That no one else frowns when I bird or I'm late,
That I am the one who determines my fate.
As I write of the joy that I've found this past year,
My day seems more lively, not nearly so drear
It may seem that all of my work's for a fee,
But in my own office, my work is for me.
Of course, by myself, I have no one to blame,
When I miss a date or misplace a name.
The blame and the credit rest solely on me,
The bad with the good in equal degree.
Humility teaches alertness and care.
Experience teaches I should not despair.
The client is told, the music is faced,
The errors explained, though never erased.
It's part of anyone's practice of law,
And life must go on, in spite of the flaw.
Tomorrow will come; I'll hold my head high.
I'm good, though not perfect, I cannot deny.

At a Continuing Legal Education Lecture (10/24/00)

It's weird to be in class again, back where I've already been.
Frenetic notes I try to take, sincerely trying to stay awake.
Daydreams brief and doodles too, lots of time with naught to do.
Apathy gradually settling down, days of green go gradually brown.
Brilliant thoughts of birds are dim. Future plans are strangely grim.

And then an interesting thought comes through. My mind alerts. My thoughts are new.
I see the slides, the topic's great, ignoring this might seal my fate.
I like this stuff. I understand! This CLE is truly grand.
So, in and out, I drift along, learning what to do and what is wrong.
It's nice to be immersed, alone, away from life and telephone.
Time to learn and time to dream; life as good as it does seem.

DAVE AND MARRIAGE

Although I wrote reams in my journals about Dave once I decided that we should be married (which occurred the day after I met him when he was a meteorology graduate student), I have not written many poems or prose about him since then, except for the following. These two poems were written to be read to the wonderful people of Community United Church of Christ, where he was the pastor, at the good-bye event that they scheduled for us.

Dave (7/18/99)

Ther once was a man, name of Dave,
To me, his last name he gave.
A weatherman, preacher
Bible-type teacher,
An introvert, being so brave.

This poem is a view from inside,
By the one who became his young bride,
He is funny and sweet,
Without lies or deceit,
And he loves his food salty and fried.

Meteorology was his first passion,
Even though' it was not always in fashion.
A man with no powers,
To come in out of the showers,
Even when the thunder is crashin'.

His reading takes up many hours,
In fact, there are books he devours,
He enjoys writing words
(a bit more than birds)
But he also has found time for flowers.

Now Dave has a passion for boats,
Really anything hull-like that floats,
As he approaches the sea,
There's a true inner glee.
It's on nautical things that he dotes.

He's really astoundingly calm.
In fact, it takes a real bomb,
To jolt him to rage,
To look up from the page,
(rather like my sweet, sainted mom).

His devotion to justice is great,
Both in marriage, and out in the state,
When a thing is unfair,
He will tear out his hair,
Which might explain his bald pate.

He loves music and joining in singing,
It is joy to the music he's bringing,
Though the notes may be wrong,
He rejoices in song,
As the music to heaven is winging.

Now listen really carefully, I implore you,
About this man who stands here before you,
He's devoted to you,
And to all that you do,
So, I'll stop here, he wouldn't want me to bore you.

BIRDING TIMES, A LIFE IN RHYMES

Dave (Tune: "Both Sides Now") (7/18/99)

Watching clouds, in Ohio, a child from boy to man did grow.
He journeyed west, to wild Mad., Wis.; he was a Methodist,
But then we met, we courted, wed; "Go west, young man", the people said,
So many places he has been, and clouds have led the way.

Chorus: He's looked at clouds through isobars, through plotting maps, beneath the stars,

But then he got the vision, call;
Became a church pastor, after all.

Anchorage and Corvallis, too. Amazing things that we went through.
Far away from home and friends, we were alone and yet,
The church helped us to see it through, then came the day a change was due,
And so, we came across the land, and so began again. **Chorus**

Though clouds and weather took the fore, the church began to be much more,
The people, CLAY, and Cally, too, they helped to shape his soul,
Deep within, a little voice, a time to make another choice,
To seminary, he did go, and did become ordained. **Chorus**

A church like this, we'd never known; the friends we've made, the time has flown;
It's quite amazing to be here, as "first lady", somehow.
One cold day past, the clouds did clear. He saw his path; it led to here.
So many things he could've done, but this is our love now. **Chorus**

Our Journey So Far (to 2000) (Tune: "Oh Susannah") (9/2000)

Oh, I come from cold Wisconsin, and he comes from Ohio,
And we first met up in Madison, so very long ago.
'Tween watching clouds and watching birds, we somehow found the time,
To meet and date each other-- and everything was fine.

Oh Wisconsin, a state we'll always love,
With birds atwittering down below, and fluffy clouds above.
We began our married life; it was in 1968,
When we took a giant trip to that great Alaskan state.
We drove a million miles, of gravel, clay and holes;
A weatherman and housewife--those were our stated goals.
Oh Alaska, so very far away;
A state of beauty, trees and birds; but we decided not to stay.
So, we landed back in Madison, with turmoil raging round.
We studied very, very hard; enlightenment was found.
We got involved at our campus church; we rode our Charlie-horse,
Then we finally got our PhD's and left again, of course.
Oh education, so very much to do.
Some facts became a part of us, and others passed on through.
Our move took us to Oregon, to start our lives anew,
We biked to work, researched and taught, and just enjoyed the view.
It rained so much in Oregon; there was no drought to fear;
The mildew grew between our toes, for nine months of the year,
Oh Corvallis, a rainy land of green,
Rainbows and beauty unsurpassed--the loveliest that I've seen.
Dave did his work on wind-flow, as it poured out 'tween the hills,
For seeing when the fields could burn, and where to put windmills.
And Lynn worked on the little bugs, that live within the soils,
And both of them were diligent as they went about their toils.
Oh academia, politics and grants,
A world of education, and ladder-climbing ants.
We began to look for other jobs, we searched the country wide.
We couldn't find a place to go with two jobs, side-by-side.
We tried the west and then the east, and finally saw a light,
We pulled up stakes and headed out, 'cause everything was right.
Oh transition, no matter where you go,
You're always in-between the ends, caught up in the flow.
So, we landed out in Raleigh, on a steamy August day,
A little dog and two of us, three thousand miles away.
We settled in and found a church, and many friends as well,
We'd found a place that seemed to fit, but only time would tell.

Oh beginnings, the world glows bright and new.
A brand-new world, exciting things are everywhere to do.
For three years Lynn did research, and played with bugs and things,
Then she did the law school bit, and all that law school brings.
Now Dave, it took him five years to become a pupil too,
And then became a pastor, without much more ado.
Oh transition, Deja vu again.
Heading out together, to where we've never been.
The years went by quite gently, fitting like a glove.
It's nice to go to work each day, just doing what you love.
Evenings filled with meetings, days whizzing by between,
But just on the horizon, a menace, yet unseen.
Oh, what joy, what beauty in the days,
But such things do not last, forever or always.
This part is quite unpleasant. Suffice it just to say,
This person came, made quite a mess, and then she went away.
The two of us dropped everything, prepared to leave the place,
Dave found a job in Texas, a hot but lovely space.
Oh y'all, come out and visit us.
We'll be extremely happy and make a joyful fuss!

ANGST, QUESTIONS AND INSPIRATION

The poems in the first set below were written in 1996 when for some unforgotten reason, I had decided to write "morning pages" every day. I made myself write, but often nothing was happening that I felt interested in writing paragraphs on. As I would sit there, stymied, a poem would often emerge. Often the words of the poem reflected my frustration that I was finding it so hard to write at all. In many of the poems selected for this section, whether the poems were part of my morning pages or were written later, there is a clear theme of worrying about being obsessive about things. One could say I was (am?) obsessed with obsessiveness. These poems often are more inward-looking than the birdy poems and the straightforward accounts of what was happening in my world.

Morning Page Poems

Snowed in in Greenville, North Carolina (1/8/96)

There once was a lawyer named Lynn,
Who waited for life to begin.
She fumed and she fussed,
Lacking wisdom and trust,
Wondering where she should go from where she had been.

And so, she wrote pages and read,
Lounging alone on her bed,
Thinking "yes" and then "no",
As she thought of the snow,
Thinking "being alive is better than dead."

Should she paint, should she play, should she write?
The answer was nowhere in sight.
Her mind was on hold,
As she looked at the cold.
It started to dawn; 'twas no longer night.

Life (1/20/96)

Life: so severe, so intense, sharp, acute,
 screaming highs,
Slow throbbing sighs.
Clenched in knots,
Lost in thoughts.
Spinning, wild
Gentle, mild.
In the end, it's love
Supreme, above.
Let go, cease.
Peace. Amen.

Fret (1/22/96)

A poem. A prayer.
I don't know what's there.
It seethes. It croons
With a mixture of tunes.
I'm helpless to know
Where it is I should go.
though there's death after life,
Can rebirth come from strife?
Will an answer be found?
Will God make a sound?
There is no way to find
Real peace of mind.
So, I write, and I fret,
With no answer yet.
I will hope. I will try.
And I guess I'll get by.
Not sure what to do,
I will muddle through.
That's the last for today.
I've got no more to say.

What Topic to Write on (3/16/96)

Perhaps birds?
No more words.
Just singing
Music bringing
Carols descending
Praise unending
Forget sorrow
Face tomorrow
Sing rejoicing
Praiseful voicing
Why the hurry?
Why the worry?
Look around.

Let joy be found.

Computers (4/29/96)

A computer does not easily fit into a poem.
It's functional, utilitarian and stodgy at best.
Yet within it lurks brilliance, emotion, design.
It can blossom and shine if put to the test.

Unfortunately, computers have minds of their own,
And wee little thingies within them reside,
Which tend to cause problems beyond rhyme or reason,
Confounding all efforts, hiding inside.

One needs to walk softly, approach them with caution,
Take nothing for granted, stay up on one's toes,
Assume that the worst will certainly happen,
That the devil and computers are similar foes.

And then if you're lucky and amazingly patient,
You might create something, the computer and you.
Of course, you might never be able to find it,
If the computer decides that its lifetime is through.

It's just like a lot of things, full of potential,
Luring us on, with a promise and smile,
If we take our precautions and do lots of backups,
The computer may help us to go the next mile.

Fuzzy (4/29/96)

Passive, tired, keeping feelings at bay,
I try to get through each night and each day,
But my brain does strange tricks and departs from its script,
It's as if resolutions have fallen and slipped.

My long-range goals are fuzzy and blurred,
My pains and griefs are far from cured.

There's something that is trying to surface, I'm certain,
But it hides behind work as a sure type of curtain.

On Stopping Daily Writing Early (5/10/96)

I can't do it. My obsessiveness wins out.
It's a matter of personal pride, that I struggle with this every day,
That I finish my pages,
Though it sometimes takes ages,
And it's often with lots of delay.

There's something within that cries out,
That needs to do this, it appears,
That needs to go on
To get the thing done,
It drives away shadows and fears.

Fifty (5/16/96)

I'm turning fifty, quite astounding.
Never thought I'd get this far.
Always thought I'd die a youngster,
Burst, then fade, a tragic star.

Life goes on in spurts and eons,
Leading somewhere, I don't know,
Bringing joys I didn't plan for,
Likewise, sorrows, depths below.

Days rush by, a blur of happenings,
Some stand out; the others fade.
People enter and leave too quickly,
All a part of the parade.

Special moments, full of wonder,
Envelope me in thanks, delight,
Giving life a touch of goodness,
Changing darkness into sight.

Sometimes I stop and look around me,
Letting senses stretch and grow,
Touching earth and heaven together,
Breathing God and letting go.

Flying (6/9/96)

Each day we are flying, in air or on land,
Quite often it's bumpy, and usually unplanned.
It seems we're in charge with our hands on the wheel,
Yet a moment's distraction, and the whole thing's unreal.
"What happened?" we ask with bewildered distress,
"Why are things upside down? Why has more turned to less?
Where has everyone gone? Did I make a wrong turn?
Was I sleeping again? Was there something to learn?"
Ignoring the answers, we rush blindly on,
Not seeing each other, not seeing the dawn.
Not waiting, not listening, not being at all,
We lunge toward the cliff, intent on the fall.
It takes something awe-full, like rainbows or death,
To make us slow down and pause for a breath,
To pull us up short, in wonder or pain,
To take time for crying, to dance in the rain.
To feel that we're part of the world, not its head,
That not only the stomach, but the soul, should be fed.
There's more to life than planning and lists,
There's laughter and puppies and sharing and mists.
There are views while we're flying and wonders untold.
We needn't stop flying to have them unfold.
We just need awareness, to open our eyes,
To feast on creation, to drink in the skies,
To see what we're doing, to see who we're being,
To look at our flight with eyes that are seeing,
So that when we're done with no more of flying,
Our hearts will know peace, a peace death-defying.

Getting Late to Daily Writing (6/26/96)

It's always late. My mind grows blank,
And it's only me I have to thank.
I could've written. I had the time.
All that comes to me now, comes out in rhyme.
Maybe my brain slipped out of gear
At this late hour, like having a beer.
The intellect leaves, the feelings thrive,
My thoughtfulness does not survive.
I think I go from "T" to "P"*
The words once hidden now burst free.
My brain is dull, my pen goes on,
Would things reverse if I wrote at dawn?
Maybe inside there are two Lynns,
When one is ending, the other begins,
Together a whole is somehow made,
It seems to be stable, so I'm not afraid
That I'll burst the seams and split into two,
Of course, if I did, there's more I could do.
*classifications in the Myers-Briggs Personality Test

Why Do I Make Myself Write Pages Each Day? (7/20/96)

I yawn, I wiggle, I'm tired of writing.
Why do I continue the struggle, the fighting?
What's the reward awaiting my hours?
Will it bring money, success, greater powers?
It's sort of a test, a discipline, trial.
Can I make myself do it, even when it seems vile?
But it's more. There's a hope of inspiring grace,
That lurking in me, in some far hidden place,
Is a fountain of wisdom, or perhaps just a trickle
That I hope will prove constant and will not turn fickle.
A genius, a spark, a creation-in-waiting,
From mere words on paper will come a creating.
I've felt it arise from my pen, unexpected,
But I need to do writing so it can be detected.

And another page looms, not a thought is appearing,
Yet the pen keeps on going, an unseen force, steering.
In rhyme, it's much easier, which seems slightly crazy.
The harder stuff, easy? I guess I'm not lazy.
It's as if there is someone, not me, who's in control here,
And my head is on idle. Perhaps it's my soul here.
Perhaps if I tried to do spiritual things,
My earth-weary body would gain spirit wings.
Perhaps if I tried in a room soul-inducing,
Creations of worth would be self-producing.
I need to take time when there's time to be taken,
And seek for myself – the road not yet taken.

Yawn (7/29/96)

Yawn. Yawn. On and on.
Where goes the day? What have I done?
The time unnoticed once again
Has passed me by. What might have been.
A couple moments carefully used.
The rest – kaput. I'm left confused.
"The best laid plans", it has been said
Could not control the time which fled.
The plan must be to pick and choose
Which moments count, and which I lose,
And what to do in those I hold,
Assuming they can be controlled.
How to apportion finite me
To longings extending infinitely,
To find an essence, without regret
For moments that I must forget.

Other Rambling Thoughts

Thoughts on Reading *One Year to Live* (7/22/97)

Where I am, I do not know. In my finger? In my toe?
Am I here, or have I gone? Maybe I have just moved on.
Breathing slowly, I come back, soften tummy, feel it slack.

Feeling joy and feeling pain, feeling things I can't explain.
In my soul, I hope to strive, to prepare for death by being alive.
In striving I will open wide, to be the self that is inside.
Striving to relax my clutch, on all the things I love so much,
All the beauty, dances, birds, all the touches and the words.
Apparently, I've always been, as I am now, so was I then.
Great, expanding, beyond time; unbound by body, soul sublime.
Gratitude, compassion, grace; I am self without my face.
Dependence on self-pride, success – replaced by love, on all to bless.

Southern Lethargy (7/25/97)

No wonder the people in the South have often lagged behind us Yanks.
So often have I prayed for warmth, yet rarely given thanks
For a crisp, cold car, for shivered morns, for icy streets, and snowy days,
Now here I sit, awash in warmth, my head is dead, I'm in a daze.
The heat has dulled my every sense, my little brain has gone astray,
I'll have to save my thinking self and bring it forth another day.

Time Out (7/26/97)

I went to the mountains, to let silence in,
It happened this morning, in air still and thin.

Apart from them all, surrounded by trees,
I began to relax, by little degrees.

As dawn filtered through, and bird songs were heard,
As a breeze gently blew, and green leaves were stirred,

I knew once again my need to be free,
For moments of time, moments for me,

Time to rejoice, time to be still,
Time for my heart and my soul to re-fill.

Glorious Day (9/14/97)

It's an ee cummings-y glorious day,
I look and I see that it's coming my way.

"There's a bright golden haze," as it says in the song,
And this is my day, all the day long.

Where will I take it? What will I do?
Actually, that sort of depends upon you –

"you" being that being I talk to inside,
That helps me make choices or not to decide.

There's a pull to do nothing, to go with the flows.
There's an opposite pull. I don't know where it goes.

This happens each day, on good days and bad—
An ongoing tension—roses? Or plaid?

Sparkling raindrops or puddles of pain?
Where this day goes, I won't know 'til I've been!

Home to Wisconsin (9/20/97)

A refluxing feeling of terror and joy
Arises and falls and rises again.
I enter the flatland, where it's fall, and I feel
Nostalgia for moments that never have been.

A world where prairies are hidden 'neath towns,
Afternoon cumuli billow above,
The world that I came from, and have never left,
The world that I fled, the world that I love.

Forced Centering (9/25/97)

I packed my book. I cannot read.
I have an hour in which to sit.

A day of sun and beauty passes.
There's little I can do with it.

I'd love to sketch, or paint a feather,
Go out walking, twirl and dance,
Fill my time with things worth doing,
Not waste time or miss a chance.

What is my problem? What's the hurry?
It doesn't hurt to sit, be still.
The time will come for all that flurry.
The time will come that I can fill.

For now, relax, breathe slow and feel that
Life is good, and should be treasured,
Feel the tension slowly draining,
Feel the time be still, unmeasured.

Feel a vow, inside me, forming:
Space is needed for my soul.
Time will tell, and time is telling.
I need the time to be made whole.

Genes (11/4/97)

What in my genes determines how I
React to the world, see through my eye?

Is there a gene for the loving of life?
Is there a gene that says "no" to strife?

Why when facing a future unknown
Do some people smile, and some people moan?

Do we learn it through our struggles on earth,
Or is it within us from the time of our birth?

Although we all must face heartache and pain,
Although there are storms and blizzards and rain,

It seems that for some the pain is decreased,
The sorrow is lessened, the anguish released.

Somehow, I see that there's good in the bad,
Growth in the pain, joy in the sad,

That although life may be pretty grim for a while,
There will be a tomorrow, and again I will smile.

Arriving in Raleigh by Plane (11/4/97)

It is beautiful below; I just woke up to find
Red, yellow, green…the north left behind.

An idyllic fall day, a day burnished gold,
A half a day left, still to unfold,

Cloud patterns of cotton, green fields below,
Dappled with shadows, a world all a-glow.

Is Nothing Right? (1998)

There's nothing seems to be just right;
The day's too cloudy, the sun's too bright.
There's not enough; there's too much food;
I want it now; not in the mood.
My life's too short; my life's too long.
There's too much quiet; there's too much song.
The room's too hot; the room's too cold.
You're way too young; you're much too old.
My life's too empty; my life's too full.
A push from here; from there a pull.
I've learned a lot since I was young,
Through many songs that I have sung.
Though gripes go on about our lot,

We'll take it still; it's all we've got.

Older (3/22/98)

"I'm older," she said, in a dreamy, still voice.
"I didn't expect it; I'd really no choice.

One day I was young, a novice, afraid,
The next I'm mature, not quite an old maid.

It seems as if whole chunks of time never were,
A fast-forward life with the future a blur.

Should I put out my foot to slow down the pace?
Should I step aside slightly, cease from the race?

As each new day dawns, as I squint in the sun,
Do I face a beginning, or a life nearly done?

It's all in perspective, in the viewpoint that's taken.
Will I doze though my life or begin to awaken?

Time is too precious; I must be alert.
Pull my head from the clouds and out of the dirt,

Experience the now, and plan to do more,
Toss out the tedious; begin to explore.

Choose in each moment, what to hold or release,
Measure out freely, aliveness and peace."

Obsessing (3/28/98)

Obsession is mine, saith Lynn, sometimes in big things, or small.
The problem is not what I obsess on, but that I'm obsessing at all.

It tends to warp what I'm thinking; my concentration is nil,
Or else concentration overpowers me, and I cannot do what I will.

Why can't I be normal, in balance?
Perhaps it has something to do with the presence, or absence, of talents,

A lack of self-moderation, a surplus of energy, life,
A need to be doing, creating; the hunger for pleasure, not strife.

Plans (5/8/98)

My life is a series of waitings, of plottings,
Of carefully laid plans.
Impatience is carefully channeled
Through multiple one-event stands.

And so, when I'm caught in a downtime,
With nothing immediate to do,
I fret and I pace and I worry,
And generally get in a stew.

All the things I have planned in the future,
Aren't ready and can't be so soon,
And the things I had planned for this instant,
Have somehow escaped to the moon.

This is the time I'd allotted to clients
And legal endeavors, for pay.
I don't feel quite free to go birding –
That wasn't the plan for today.

Rigidity structures the moments
And keeps spontaneity at bay.
Who cares? When my planning is thwarted,
I guess it is now time to play.

Bedtime Prayer (7/6/98)

Creativity often brings on dreams,
Or so it often to me seems.

So, I'll write this verse and hope and pray
That dreams will come before the day.

Need (7/18/98)

I need to buy a book today,
That will speak to the sound of my soul,
I need to get away, away,
And work to make myself whole.

Sacredness (7/25/98) (driving to Morehead to bird)

Where do I draw the line between the sacred and the rest?
What makes the one thing holy, but the others not so blest?

Are human beings different from the world of living things?
Do I draw the line at mammals, or at little birds with wings?

And what about the flowers, and what about the earth?
Are some things of great value, and others of no worth?

What makes us think we're special, endowed with special grace?
What elevates our species to an exalted place?

The wondrous brains we're given that set us so apart
Have caused our eyes to cease to see, have hardened what was heart.

With the special gifts we're given, there comes a special role,
To love the earth entirely, and the creation as a whole!

Lost Direction (4/5/99)

I think I've lost direction. My rudder's sort of loose.
The things that I have tried are really not much use.

A thousand things are calling. I strain to find a clue
Of where I should be going, of what I'm called to do.

I hasten toward a goal; am brought up short, non-plussed.
What once was felt as need no longer is a must.

It's easy to ignore it, to go on as before
But if I stop and ponder, I know there must be more.

How does one know the answer? And will I ever know
What really is my calling, the way that I should go?

Utopia? (4/5/99)

There's a yearning deep inside me for a world that's felt, not seen,
A world of joy in living in a place I've never been.

In that land are many cultures; I can help them if I try.
There's beauty all-surrounding, through which each of us can fly.

We are all in this together, as we work to ease the pain,
There's no need to hoard or hurt in a race for our own gain.

We each know that there's no boundary that exists between our souls.
In that world we love each other in our many, varied roles.

There's an omnipresent purpose that all life be filled with peace,
And a knowledge that with death, we will find a sure release

From all that could be harmful, or could threaten who we are,
And that life and death give glimpses through a heaven-door, ajar.

And? (4/6/99)

Loss of innocence, bemoaned.
Where life's found can also be
Deep despair, deceit and anger,
Cruelty, insanity.

So, I seek to fill my moments
Full of beauty, wonder, grace,

Newborn things, an act of kindness
Sunlit dawn, a radiant face.

Deep absorption in the movement:
Feel the music, live the dance.
Hold the wonder, lose agendas.
Give a burst of joy a chance.

Embracing Life (5/2/99)

It seems the truth: there are very few who, feeling joy, embrace their life.
It may be that the joy supply is sparser than the rampant strife.

I really don't know any way to make it through the dismal days,
Except to hurry through the dark, emerging where the sunlight plays.

My light reserves decay with time. With gross neglect they might be lost.
I need to put behind what's gone, and nurture hope, at any cost.

When eyes are shut, or backward turned, it's difficult to find the trail.
It's difficult to even look. It's so much easier to fail.

Though failure has its own reward in reconfirming lack of worth,
There's so much more to do and be if we seek life and bold rebirth.

I need to practice what I preach. I need to extricate my soul
From places where it slowly dies. A life that's LIVED should be my goal.

Where Are We Going? (8/7/99) Written 2 weeks after Dave announced his resignation from his Raleigh pastor position.

The house is a mess.
The future unknown.
The years we've lived here-
Don't know where they've gone.

I face to the west.
Will we follow the sun?
Or head back home
To where we've begun?

What about New England-
Boston or Maine?
Or Charlottesville?
Are we hoping in vain?

What we need are birds
And a church we could love,
And a whole lot of help
From the heavens above.

Gray Hair (10/11/99)

When I was a child, I looked like a child,
I behaved as a child, though not really wild.

But when I got older, my age got ahead.
"I thought you were younger," everyone said.

I kept striving to look as old as my peers,
But my face and behavior subtracted the years.

And then one day, my age crossed the line
And the appearance of youngness was really quite fine.

BIRDING TIMES, A LIFE IN RHYMES

I delighted in surprising the new friends I made
By disclosing my age (by my face not displayed).

That time then went past; I got wrinkles, gray hairs,
My gait was slowed down, especially up stairs.

But just now I noticed my appearance is ahead
As a wee bit of elegance silvers my head.

As my look of maturity is gradually unfurled
It's a young me inside me encountering the world.

I still run and dance. I still jump and shout,
As a little old lady lets the little girl out.

At heart, I am young, whatever my face,
Exuberant about living in this time and place.

Uncertain (awaiting whether Ft. Worth, Albuquerque or somewhere else will be our new home) (11/12/99)

It's so easy, as day follows day
To ignore the time that is passing away,

To take for granted that morning will come,
To see the sun set, with the mind gone numb.

When something happens to jolt me awake,
When a once-planned future goes sadly opaque,

It's then that I know that nothing is clear.
Precise future plans are figments of fear.

The need to be certain, at each step I take,
To know where I'm going as the past I forsake

Compels me to fashion, so I will not fail,
A plan I can follow, in every detail.

Reality, unfortunately, has again reared its head.
I have no real clue to what lies ahead.

There are multiple pathways, truly a maze.
The answer lies hidden in thick swirling haze.

Plans (11/26/99)

Fort Worth
Such mirth.
Forthwith, we'll be there.
Such pain,
All the rain.
Our last days here – 'tisn't fair.

Knitting
Sitting,
What should I do?
Wording,
Birding,
Choices, few.

Clouded,
Shrouded,
Gray and Gloom,
Dancing,
Prancing,
There's no room.

Drizzle,
Fizzle,
Plans are changed,
"Non-bucketacious"
Quite outrageous,
We're deranged.

Bemoaning Time (1/24/01)

Our lives are so short, and there's so much to do,
And always the yearning to find something new.

The need to create bubbles through me, and then
Recedes into longing for what has not been.

There are pictures to take and to paint and to see,
Beauty to find and to touch and to be,

Songs to be played, to be sung, to be danced,
Tension removed and vision enhanced.

All I know is unless I break free of my chain,
I will always be yearning, always in pain.

Aging (tune: "Mine Eyes Have Seen the Glory…") (9/21/07)

I've begun to see the wrinkles, and I've seen the graying hair.
It's the end of what was middle age. It really isn't fair.
My mind wants to begin things, but my body isn't there.
Am I coming or am I going?

Goodness, gracious, though it seems I've just begun,
My bones are aching as if the race was run.
Although at times I've faltered, on the whole it has been fun.
It's time to sing out thanks.

Between the start and finish, it can be a scary trail.
It's not clear what is happening – will we succeed or fail?
Will we reach our destinations, not get swallowed by the whale?
But we keep on keeping on.

Goodness, gracious, dear God to you I pray,
Give me strength to start, and to end each day.
Guide my footsteps, as I travel on my way.
And thank you for your light.

LYNN E. BARBER

Where (7/12/09) (no idea where the following came from)

Where are you going, little one, little one?
Where are you going, with your limp and your cane?
Turn around and you're young, turn around and you're old,
Do you know where you're going? Don't go there again.

Dirt (4/5/09, I think)

I just can't write a poem about dirt.
Dirt is too dingy, drab, dusty, depressing.
Clinging cloyingly closely to clothing,
Filling every imaginable opening.
I just can't write about dirt.

Doctor's Office (4/7/09, I think) (not a rhyme; a pre-pandemic worry)

I sit in the doctor's waiting room.
The cold clean medical instruments lined up in a row ready for action.
The shiny bottles and tubes leering at me from across the countertop.
The walls are scrubbed, the floor just vacuumed, the adjustable chair for me wiped clean.
Even the tissue box seems to have been polished.
It all seems so sterile and aseptic,
But on the wrinkled magazine cover,
A germ lingers,
Waiting,
Waiting,
For the chance of a lifetime.

Morning Routine (4/8/09, I think)

Dog out, dog in,
That's the way my days begin.

Feed the dog, water too.
Such exciting things to do.

Shower, brush, get dressed,
Not the things that I like best.

It gets better – break the fast,
Eat enough, it's got to last.

So, it goes. What a bore.
I'm so glad there's something more.

Friday (4/10/09, I think)

Friday had always been overrated.
It gives me an ulcer to contemplate it.
All week long I procrastinated,
And when Friday arrived, I was devastated.

I still had tons of stuff to do.
There was no way that I was through.
So, I could not go home, I was so blue,
And my phobia about Fridays grew and grew.

The Greenhouse (4/11/09)

I sit in the garden alone,
A greenhouse, where nothing is grown,
On its benches sit pots,
And various what-nots,
But its days of glory have flown.

There really is no longer room.
For seedlings or flowers in bloom.
The parallel to me
Is striking to see,
A source of depression and gloom.

Perhaps if I cleaned up the mess,
It would result in reduction of stress,
But that's for tomorrow.
Let me wallow in sorrow,
Which cheers me up, or didn't you guess?

More Self-analysis (4/09)

There's a small part of me that wants to go home,
Put my head under the covers and never come out.
But there certainly is another part,
That wants to wield power and have a big clout.

Rant Rant (1/17/10, I think)

There's something demoralizing about being around people
Who always are negative, who rail and rant.
People who rarely say words of approval.
They never say, "do it", but instead they say, "can't".

There are people who begin nearly all conversations
By criticizing someone or something they've done,
People who live to deflate all your bubbles,
People who revel in hiding the sun.

I don't see the point in bringing down others,
Or in niggling or making degrading remarks.
Much better to put out the fires when we see them,
Than to form little flames and spread dangerous sparks.

How? (5/15/10)

How many years do I have left to me?
How many birds do I have left to see?

How will I know that I've naught left to do?
How will I know that my living is through?

How can I stand to stand still and not try
To do one more thing, before I must die?

The longer I live, the more that I know,
I've things I must do, and places to go.

I've paintings to paint, and songs I must sing,
There are projects undone, and birds beckoning.

On a drive from Rockport to Home (9/18/10)

Is it the age of my friends, or the age of me?
When they look in my eyes, what do they see?

With hardly a thought, our words turn to death,
About will we be ready to take our last breath.

It is so hard to know that I'm on the downslope,
To say goodbye to some visions and lower some hope.

The odd thing is that most of the time,
Life's pretty good, close to sublime.

Except when escaping from my careful control,
Out pops a fear that rattles my soul.

Choices (at age 64) (10/6/10)

What to do when the future's uncertain:
Make lots of lists, considering choices.
What to do in the midst of cacophony:
Try to rule out the negative voices.

It's sad to find out that the path is divided,
The path that I'm on and the one not yet taken.
Why am I not a bit more amoeboid?
It could help resolve a life that is shaken.

Okay – so I'll handle another complexity.
I'll live in a world disjointed, unknown.
Perhaps it will help me finally decipher,
What I will do when at last I am grown.

Driving (11/7/10) I was unable to move to South Dakota in late 2010 when Dave got a job there. My term as president of The Texas Ornithological Society ended in May of 2011 and I was determined to stay until it was done. My second book also came out in the spring of 2011 at Texas A&M University Press, and I had scheduled numerous Texas bird club talks about it. Shar in the following poem is our dog at that time.

Driving and driving and driving some more,
(I'm sure Shar is wondering what it's all for).

It's part of the weirdness I'm sure that I face.
My life is suspended in more than one place.

My future, while hopeful, is completely a blur.
Will I move? Will I stay? Nothing is sure,

Except, I will bird, wherever I go,
And wherever Dave goes, eventually, I'll go.

Driving to College Station to Pick Up More of My Books (5/23/11)
Hearing about Joplin, MO tornado.

How to balance the need to help birds
With tornados' destruction more awful than words,

With floods that are covering the homes and the land,
When all things are chaos, and naught is as planned.

Do we throw up our hands over loss of control?
Do the horrors around rob our life of its soul?

While the temptation is great to abandon it all,
To give up on the helpless, the threatened, the small,

I still feel the need to reach out and to try,
To rescue the hope and help it to fly.

Moving – Fort Worth to Rapid City (9/19/11)

Shifting my allegiance – what makes it happen so?
When it came the time for moving, I didn't want to go.

Yet, flying out of Dallas, I'm yearning for the hills,
For rolling golden prairie, for gentle yard-bird thrills.

Perhaps I need uprooting from things I've grown to love.
To broaden my horizons, I need a little shove.

The problem is the people who've made my world a home,
It's very hard to leave them, when comes the time to roam.

It's hard to stay connected when I'm so far away,
When life is full of new things that fill up every day.

Uncertainty (9/21/12)

Whatever happened to days that were certain?
When living felt safe, and nothing was hurting.

I'm afraid that it all was just an illusion,
That blinders concealed a world of confusion.

I usually think that I'm in control of tomorrow:
I can plan for the joy and limit the sorrow.

But then there are times when I know that I lack
Any clue of what's happening, and I want to go back

To life that is sheltered, prescribed and well-known,
Where paths are well-trod and I'm never alone.

New Year's Resolutions (12/27/20) In contemplating writing my moderator's article for the January 2021 First Congregational Church (Anchorage) newsletter, the only things I could think of were that 2020 was nearly over, the pandemic was still here, and for 2021 I needed to think of New Year's resolutions. For some reason my thoughts came out in the following doggerel.

New Year's resolutions? How silly it seems.
What can I plan for? What's in my dreams?

My own little world is encompassed by Zoom.
Outside of Zoom boxes is left little room

For imagining what I might endeavor to be,
If ever from Covid my life is set free.

I know in the future something "normal" will rise.
Until then 'midst all of world's sorrows and cries,

I'll try to be better, be kinder, more nice.
As for future control, it's a roll of the dice.

Yet I'm hopeful in rather the optimist's way,
That life will be better – 'twill be a new day.

Every day is precious, no matter the date-
My new resolution – to celebrate! Happy New Year!!

House-hunting (3/7/21) Dave had decided to retire in early 2021. After much discussion, we decided to try to find a house in Wisconsin for us to move to what would hopefully be our last house. Because of the ongoing pandemic and the distance from Alaska to anywhere else, we did not feel free to travel there to look at houses, so we enlisted the long-distance help of a Wisconsin realtor who gave us virtual tours of a number of houses. The biggest problem was that everyone else also appeared to be house-hunting, and we just could not find a house and make an acceptable offer rapidly enough to land a deal. While feeling a strong pull to move south, I very much also did not want to leave Alaska, primarily because of close friendships there.

I'm hoping that they will say yes,
But fearing that they will say no.
What will occur
If they choose to demur,
And where on earth will we go?

Time has passed, and the answer was "no",
Which made me scream and be teary,
But we're looking again,
Though not knowing when
A house will again make us cheery.

As a Child (3/10/21)

When I was a child, I wrote as a child,
With words that were simple, guileless and true.

Now that I'm older, much older, I hope that
Truth will still manage somehow to come through.

Yearning (3/13/21)

To yearn for two things that both cannot be,
To pine both for forest and also for sea,

Where there are mountains, I also need plains,
Where there are blue skies, I'm missing the rains.

I want to be at all the places I've been
But this is now, and those were then.

I need to be present to the now, to the here,
And also hold fast to the memories so dear.

Waiting to Know the Future (3/30/21)

Waiting is something that I hate. Waiting stabs my soul.
Waiting chills and waiting burns. Waiting's fire and I'm the coal.

Awaiting good things should be fun, but there's a dread I feel inside.
Something bad will intervene, and all the good will be denied.

Awaiting bad things should be better – maybe they also are not sure,
Yet I also know without a doubt, even worse things may occur.

So I am for a little less waiting, for things to happen with a little more speed.
A life of pleasant anticipation – it's clear that this is what I need.

On a lighter note, but more wishful thinking (3/31/21)

There once was a birder named Lynn,
I don't know just where to begin,
She was carried away
By an eagle one day –
She was so incredibly thin.

Many Boxes (to the tune of "Little Boxes") (5/2/21) (as we packed for our move from Alaska to Wisconsin)

There are boxes all around the house, there are boxes made of cardboard,
There are boxes all around the house, there are boxes, not the same.

There's a big one, filled with blankets, and a small one, filled with spice jars,
And many heavy boxes, filled with books of every kind.

There are rakes and hoes and shovels, and feeders for the little birds,
And many fragile things that the movers soon will pack.

There are boxes out in the garage, and boxes in the hallway,
And boxes everywhere you look, helter, skelter, everywhere.

And their owners are a lawyer (and birder and biologist)
And pastor (and weatherman) – a most eclectic pair.

They are all going to Wisconsin, and leaving their Alaska home
On a journey, long and winding, over mountains and the plains.

And they're hoping that the closing will be scheduled in a couple days,
Otherwise, all these boxes may wind up in the street.

Nap (7/17/21)

"Lie down for a nap? Out of the question".
That was before we retired in May.
Now it's become surprisingly useful
To do a "drop down" in the shank of the day.

Need to Do Something (8/10/21)

Each of us is centered in our own universe.
Each of us trying to not make things worse.

All around us is hatred and grief.
What can we do to help bring relief?

The temptation is strong to close our eyes and our ears,
To retreat from it all, to lessen our fears.

In spite of the agony, sorrow and pain,
We all must do something to keep ourselves sane.

We really can't stay in our own little bubbles.
It's time to do something to lessen the troubles.

Even if what we attempt seems so small,
It's better than doing nothing at all.

Five Months Ago (10/17/21)

Seventy-five, and still alive! An amazing thing I say.
Keeping going, never knowing, that I would reach that day.

I started small (don't we all) in Wausau, don'tcha know?
The years have passed, really fast, not ever going slow.

A world of four, not wanting more, but then the birds arrived.
Without that love, around, above, I wouldn't have survived.

Each grassy lane that kept me sane, each field, each bush, each tree,
Each open space, each leafy place, held birds that sang to me.

The lens of birds, that focused words, that brought me to the now
Through these glasses, I took classes, though it worked I know not how.

Long years reading, only needing time outdoors to keep life glistening.
Times for looks away from books, times for seeking and for listening.

Also, lists of birds not missed, birds of wonder, birds of glory,
Birds inspired, birds desired, birds that now comprise my story.

Were there the days I withheld praise? Days when things did not go right?
More than one, yet when all's done, darkness always turned to light.

All my life, in joy, in strife, has been about me and birds,
But starting now, I hope and vow to do good things with actions, words.

   Purple Potato (11/20/21) Thanks to Ellen and Fred, our friends from college, who welcomed us back to Wisconsin in 2021, with meals halfway between our homes and lovely gifts of the purple potatoes that they grew in great abundance.

Purple potato salad, with eggs and onions too.
More purple potatoes in a yummy vege stew.

Each of them a gift from Ellen and from Fred.
Excellent additions to our daily bread.

Contemplating the Future (11/30/21)

A molecule of me (after I am gone)
Hovers o'er the page that you are reading on.

I wonder where it's been since my passing day.
Has it had a life of unrestricted play?

Has it traveled far? Does it have a clue
That as you read these words, I am meeting you.

Glass Half Empty or Half Full (8/16/24)

I just can't keep standing; the world swirls around.
I feel like I'm screaming, but don't make a sound.

My body is aching. My muscles complain.
Overwhelming, the tiredness. Enmeshed in the pain.

I must close my eyes, make the fog go away.
But I have the scared feeling that it's all here to stay.

I lift my head slowly. The world is not spinning!
So, I guess it's not ending. At worst, it's beginning.

DEATH AND DYING

Death and Life and Death (7/23/24) I am, or I at least try to be, a glass half-full person as in this most recent poem on death, but in the other previously written poems that follow it, it is clear that has been a difficult status for me to maintain.

I am lying in bed. The sky is now lightening.
My thoughts turn to death. They are calm and not frightening.
Suddenly a Cardinal sings, loud and so cheery.
No longer looking inward, my eyes become teary.
I once was convinced I'd die young, oh so tragic,
But I kept right on living – it seemed just like magic.
My awareness of death, barely felt, always known,
Had made me love life through the years that have flown.
Has made me cling tightly to the days that remain.
"Amazing is life," is my constant refrain.

My parents… My mother got cancer, went through chemo, got better, and then it came back in the mid 90's. I flew from North Carolina to Wisconsin on a regular basis during this time, which gave me much time to think about my parents and my life as a whole. It also gave me time to write poems, many of them, most of them, about my parents. It gave me time to think about the rest of my life, and eventually to reach a decision to leave a very wonderful law firm and start a solo law practice and work from home. Looking over these poems nearly 30 years later, I immediately relive the sorrow, the ups and downs, and more downs. I have included most of the poems that I wrote during that time because of how important it was for me to write them and to have written them, a way to remember.

On a Plane Scheduled to go from RDU to Wisconsin (12/30/95)

A blue-gray-yellow-pink dawn,
The plane's wings glitter with deicer.
As I sit and wait for the trip to move on,
The sky lightens; the day gets nicer.

BIRDING TIMES, A LIFE IN RHYMES

My mind's full of owls and feathered things,
And food, like warm luscious bread,
As I think of home, my heart sort of sings,
Although I admit, there's a small part of dread.

How will they be? Will they still be "all right"?
Or will it be clear that the end's very soon?
Will the days seem to dawn, or will they stay night?
Will my song turn to dirge, or to spry little tune?

The ground rushes by, and we're up in the air.
A lake glints below, surrounded by trees.
It is beautiful here; hope it's beautiful there,
Where the world sits in stillness, locked in the freeze.

I try to relax as the first leg begins
Of my trip to the far frozen north.
With my camera, my scope, my notebook and "bins"
I'm as ready as ever – and I now sally forth.

Dying (1/31/96)

My mother is dying, I scream in silence.
It's not really happening. It must be a dream.
But I know deep inside, with an absolute sureness,
That things are exactly as bad as they seem.

A sadness, emptiness, wringing heart,
Unable to be aware, to cope.
My head's full of sleep, my eyes are dull.
My spirit is failing for lack of hope.

There is nothing we do that really matters.
We've tried everything, but we can't stop the pain.
We are simply waiting and hurting together.
We don't understand. We can't explain.

I know that these days are part of living,
Yet everything now seems to be on hold.
We know that it's part of the fabric we're weaving,
But it's ugly and crooked and grim to behold.

Perhaps someday I'll see the pattern;
The whole fabric may someday appear.
I cling to that vision, and hope that the beauty
Of life, once more, will be present and clear.

She's Dying (2/3/96)

Not knowing. Denying.
Screaming. Crying.
Escaping. Flying.
Mama's dying.
Life-depressing.
Scary, stressing.
So, confessing,
Seek a blessing.

Sigh (2/8/96)

A flibbertigibbet, unstable, in flight
A need for new scenery, for fresh air and light.

There's something unnerving about sitting inside.
I need to go somewhere to walk, take a ride

Where birds could be present or something occur,
A hawk or an owl I'd really prefer.

Instead, I breathe garlic, and heave a great sigh,
Kissing wandering and beauty a tearful good-by.

Telling myself that when these days are past,
I may have more freedom for birding, at last.

So, wrapped in despair, my heart full of lead,
I contemplate Mama, asleep in her bed.

She doesn't have freedom; she can't even die.
God knows that she's tried and continues to try.

My little complaints should be shelved, that I know.
I should try to be patient, to go with the flow.

But my entire being is screaming to leave,
To find me a space where my spirit can grieve.

Here, where there's people, I must hold myself in.
I can't give in to crying. I dare not begin.

I'm afraid that I'd shatter, my heart would explode.
I'd be no help at all, could not shoulder the load.

But meanwhile, I'm gradually turning to stone,
Lost, and afraid, and feeling alone.

There's only one person in this house I could tell,
She is also alone, dying, unwell.

Of all of these people, she would say "let her bird."
But she's lost in her darkness, not saying a word.

So, we each struggle on, together, alone,
In living and dying, I cannot condone.

We cannot show more. We can't share our pain.
Our grief must be private, our grieving in vain.

We each are an island, with a moat and a wall,
Sharing glimpses of sorrow, nothing more, that is all.

LYNN E. BARBER

Harboring grudges, picking small fights,
Spoiling our days and ruining our nights.

Each lost in our anguish, but not giving in,
Not sharing ourselves. Living in sin.

The end, it will come. Will we go separate ways?
Will there be nothing to show for these horrible days?

Will we have to go on, with our separate sorrow?
Hating today and dreading tomorrow?

Not living our lives, our spirits destroyed,
Our minds in a vacuum, our souls in a void?

Is there no other choice in this world full of choices?
Is there only one way? Can't there be other voices?

Can't we share what we're feeling, live midst the dying?
Wake our cold hearts? Purge them by crying?

You'd think we were British, stiff upper lip,
Holding tight to ourselves, a very firm grip.

We need to have space, be it here or outside,
We need to be freed, no longer to hide.

We need to express, to break forth into rage,
Give vent to our feelings, rattle our cage.

It won't solve the problems; it won't be a cure,
Yet needed it is. Of that, I am sure.

So, I guess I'll keep trying, keep plugging away,
Try to have hope, continue to pray.

Life and Death (2/9/96)

Each landscape we see is both living and dead:
Oak leaves, brown and wrinkled, and needles of green.
I see Blue Jays screaming, nuthatches and crows,
But cells out there dying cannot be seen.

I can't understand why we focus on life,
Ignoring the dying, deceased and decayed,
Until one we love is facing the end,
And all of a sudden, our hearts are afraid.

Why can't we see that they're part of the whole?
Life isn't life, unless there is death.
Why can't we see that our life has its meaning
Because our heart beats, because we have breath?

All that we have is a limited time.
Whatever we do, we someday will die.
There's death all around, within and before us,
Accenting our lives, while making us cry.

I look at the birds, with their double-quick lives,
Clearly not stopping to worry and fret.
The lessons they teach as I think about dying:
Learn to live life, but do not forget.

Remember the dead and remember the living.
Rejoice while we live, and do not despair,
Live life to the full; do not waste precious moments.
Because we will die, life is holy and rare.

After (flying from Raleigh to Mosinee) (2/19/96) This was written on the day of my mother's death.

City lights glowing far down below.
They can't reach my heart; they can't dull the pain.
There's numbness, engulfing, threatening me so,
So much is lost, with nothing a gain.

How do I face the loss of a friend?
Emptiness swirls, the future is black.
The bright days are finished, hope at an end.
I'd give everything now to bring Mama back.

She knew we'd be lonely. She knew of our fears.
She tried to prepare us, to show us the way.
Yet try as I might, I can't stop the tears.
I can't stop the yearning for times far away.

I can't hug her now. I can't show her birds.
There's nothing on earth that will bring her to life.
I need to remember. I must find the words
To make sense of death and lessen the strife.

She's in me I know. She's part of me now.
For better or worse, I'm her daughter, alive.
Whatever I do, wherever I go,
Her goodness, her strength, will help me survive.

So somehow, she lives in the people she knew,
A part of her being, held onto, is saved,
Somehow, we'll go on, know what to do.
Her courage, her faith, a lesson engraved.

After (2/21/96)

My life still unlived, I tentatively plan.
Can I really begin to dream and to live?
Will my life ever seem really normal again?
Can I face God again, and learn to forgive?

Can I go on from here, or will I hold back in fear?
Can I reach for the sky for a future that's bright?
There's no way to know if I don't even try,
It will always seem dark unless I reach for the light.

Pain (3/20/96)

Feeling crappy still. Every muscle achy, moaning.
Piercing pain right from the bone.
Mama too was wracked with pain.
In my pain, I'm not alone.

Things are swirling, slipping sideways,
My orientation's gone askew.
What's the problem, you might ask.
The only answer: it's just the flu.

Going home – and Daddy (3/28/96)

There are glimpses of our likeness,
In our spirits, restless, wild.
I can feel it as I watch him.
I observed it as a child.

Though our lives are vastly different,
And our hopes and dreams diverge,
We each yearn to have a being
Where our lives and dreams can merge.

I keep hoping I will find it,
And perhaps he once did too.
Now his life has lost its focus.
There is nothing he can do.

I keep hoping I can help him
Face the empty dreaded days,
Find a light where all is darkness,
Find a path within the maze.

I have no answers, no solutions,
No idea what I should do.
Not a clue if there is something
That will help to pull him through.

I just guess I'll be myself,
Plus an extra touch of care,
Help him know that there is someone
Who's aware of his despair.

Who is also lost and lonely,
Strangely caught in skeins of grief,
Though amid a life of good things,
Quite unsure there is relief.

Maybe we can help each other,
The unseeing and the blind,
Neither knowing what we're needing,
Quite uncertain what we'll find.

There's no shortcut, no pat answer,
No safe haven, warm, secure.
Day by day we have to venture,
Find our future and endure.

We do not have our own tradition
Of reaching out or seeking aid,
Of admitting our dependence,
Of confessing we're afraid.

We're unused to in-depth sharing,
More at ease with wit and brain,
Quite unsure it's really needed
That the other know our pain.

An uphill battle lies before us,
Finding life in spite of death.
I don't know if we will make it,
But it's worth our every breath!

Thinking of Daddy's Loss (4/7/96)

I think of my life and the things that have meaning,
The things I hold on to, that make life go on.
I can't imagine if all of it vanished,
The people, the hobbies, all of them gone.

Life is so full, a rainbow of treasure.
It fills and surrounds and beckons each day.
A million small things bring light to my eyes.
They cause me to smile, to listen, to play.

How would it be if there was nothing to live for,
If the sum of my life disappeared without trace?
What would I do to keep from collapsing,
To fill up the void, to put in its place?

The moral, I think, is to live life to its fullest,
Perhaps it would help to lessen the sorrow,
Find plenty of things that bring beauty and hope,
Bring the good of the past to brighten tomorrow.

LYNN E. BARBER

Running (4/18/96)

Spread out in millions of different directions,
Running first one way, then off in another.
I know that my running helps keep thoughts at bay,
The thoughts of creation, of living, my mother.

The places I'm running – all seem quite important,
And some of them are, as I change my career,
But others are simply a means of distraction,
A way to stop sadness, stop pain and stop fear.

When I bird, I stop running, or run for pure pleasure,
I do it to do it, an end on its own,
Absorbing, fulfilling, reviving, uplifting,
My heart soars on wings, where raptors have flown.

I'm lost in the beauty, the splendor of nature,
A sensation unequalled envelops my soul,
Once again life regains its lost meaning,
The fragments, once splintered, are part of a whole.

Contemplating the Past Months after the Death of My Mother in February (10/25/96)

Our time on earth, as aliens, alone –
We strive to make contact, establish a space.
We grasp at the love and the warmth if we can,
Obsessed that we're losing an unwanted race.

Our life hurtles by us; it's out of control,
Awareness of loving arrived at too late.
Desperate, we cling to one who is dying
As grimly we grapple with knowledge of fate.

In sheer random terror, we try to find something,
To bring us to peace, to help us forget.
We plunge into life in the hope that we'll find it,
Or withdraw from the turmoil, the pain and the threat.

Death, while removing a loved one forever
Helps us reach out, bridges the gap,
Helps us to value this life and to live it,
To travel the road, lacking compass and map.

Missing Her (10/31/97)

On a plane, once again
For Chicago and onward then.

Same old trip, same old me
Doing what I oughta be.

Slowly surface age-old fears,
Missing Mama, feeling tears,

Some are dying, some are living.
All the while we need forgiving.

Caught between the future, past,
Knowing "now" can never last.

Denial - Two Years after Her Death (2/20/98)

Well, I've finished my reading, I'm ready to write,
Although no ideas have come into sight.

I'm glad to be heading up north for a while,
In spite of still being lost in denial.

Denial that Mama won't be there for me,
Denial that birding is all I can see.

Denial that Daddy is failing and old.
Denial that someday my home will be sold.

Denial that life is out of control.
Denial of being in search for my soul.

Denial that good things do come to an end.
Denial that denying is part of my trend.

My heart has grown heavy, I'm sighing, bemused.
I don't really know and am clearly confused.

Why does the process of dying and age,
Fill me with shock and smoldering rage?

It shouldn't surprise me; I've known it for years,
Yet the thought of it, always, brings me to tears.

Why can't I handle a mere fact of life?
Why should life's ending occasion such strife?

Especially the life of a person who died
With peace and her family at her bedside.

Some of it's mourning my aging, my death,
As if her last breathing became my last breath.

Part of it's losing the one person who
So clearly rejoiced in what I could do.

As if by her living my life through my tales,
She joined us together, and here myself fails.

I somehow am sure that part of her still
Remains part of me, and forever will.

BIRDING TIMES, A LIFE IN RHYMES

It's not just the genes, or the history we share,
It's more metaphysical, not here or there.

I see her in sunsets; I hear her in streams.
I know her in living; she's part of my dreams.

Her wondering love for her daughter and friend
Is something that dying has not caused to end.

Daddy (8/10/98) Flying home to Wisconsin, near the end; he died August 19, 1998.

Above the clouds we fly along.
The sky is blue, but there's no song.

My heart is empty, my mind is bare,
Between two worlds, not here nor there.

The one is full of life and birds,
The other, silent, crying words.

I yearn to flee, to hide my head,
I face the future, filled with dread.

I can't escape, I must go on
To face his dying, and when he's gone,

An end of endings; an end of me?
What happens now? Will time still be?

I take deep breaths to calm my fears,
I try to keep away the tears.

My home, my anchor, since my birth,
My validation, sense of worth.

Though when he's gone, I'll be set free,
Released from all that I "should" be.

I fear that I'll be swept away,
Deprived of laughter, light and day.

Cut off from home, without protection,
Without a map or clear direction,

A central part of what is me
Will vanish very certainly.

After (8/24/98)

I've looked for God in sunsets.
I've looked for God my whole life long.
Sometimes I feel that God appears
Whenever something could go wrong.

Depression (9/9/98)

Flying from CWA to ORD with Dave,
One moment of many that I cannot save.

I think I'm in shock and just muddling through,
Doing the things that I need to do.

I think it's the tasks that are keeping me sane,
Dimming my memory, muffling the pain.

When I surface again, emerge from the cloud,
I'm afraid I'll be cloaked by a dark, gloomy shroud,

Afraid I'll be empty, lost and forlorn,
Embracing despair that once I'd forsworn,

Afraid that depression will strangle my soul,
My series of losses taking their toll.

Decisions, Decisions (11/6/98)

Again, at an airport, the only place where
I find time to pause with a moment to spare.

Collapsed in my seat, all the hurrying done,
I gaze out the window, awaiting the sun.

This isn't a trip to a far birding spot.
Twill probably be boring, as likely as not.

Instead, we'll be slogging (that's Annie and I),
Through heaps of belongings piled high to the sky.

A million decisions as to what we should do,
Who will get what? Will we ever be through?

When we finally emerge from this mopping up phase,
When we finally escape this unending maze,

Will we know what to do when we're suddenly free?
When there's nothing between us and the clear certainty,

That Mama and Daddy and our home and our past
Are finished and gone. And the future, while vast

Seems strangely depleted, is scary, unsure,
Missing its center, robbed of allure.

Our anchor pulled up, our tether untied,
Adrift in the future, a pawn on the tide.

Home Alone (1/14/99)

Home alone. But home is fading.
There's nothing here but stuff and dreams.
The laughter, tears, the pain and sorrow
Have evanesced, or so it seems.

Inside I'm vacant, weeping, lost.
Not knowing how to leave the dead.
Trying to touch the past that's vanished.
Torn between despair and dread.

It seems so trite to lose one's parents.
So unremarkable, stale, mundane
Yet far beyond all else that's happened,
This happening brings severest pain.

A part of me is shattered, broken.
Flung on the floor, awaiting death.
Without a hope, despondent, sighing
Unaware of life and breath.

Is there any chance that I'll recover?
Emerge from now to brighter day?
Escape the tightened knot of past?
I cannot know; can only pray.

A claustrophobia wraps around me,
Terror, screaming, I cannot breathe!
Oh God, I pray for your great mercy-
My grieving and my fear relieve!

Annie (5/9/99)

I really can't write about Annie
As she stares through the glass at my plane.
Though she's stubborn as dirt,
and we often are hurt,
All I see when I look now is pain.

We seem so alone in this world.
Our world as we knew it is lost.
We spit and we fight
as we try to unite,
Ignoring the terrible cost.

We're totally different people,
As is constantly being made clear.
Where she's curly, I'm straight,
When I'm early she's late,
Things one says, the other can't hear.

We have shared so much laughter and sorrow,
And I think that we both really care.
No father, no mother.
We must cling to each other,
Not losing ourselves in despair.

I hope that somehow, we'll survive
Through the problems the future will bring,
That we'll work to be friends,
If needed, make amends,
And perhaps even laughter will ring.

After a Birding Trip (unfinished) (5/25/99)

I've just been on a birding trip, and now I'm on a plane,
Arizona behind me, Raleigh, soon again.

Counting up the birds, wishing she could know,
Wondering if she sees what's happening here "below."

Feeling she is with me, feeling she is near,
Somehow, I still wonder, what it is I fear.

She isn't there to turn to. She isn't coming back.
There's nothing she can give me of those things that I lack.

I only have the memories, and those are hard at times…

Fall (8/23/24)

One of these Falls will be my last Fall.
No more fleeting beauty. That will be all.

Right now, I must look around. Be aware.
Someday I will no longer be there.
My mind is a kaleidoscope of scenes from my past.
Like the parts of my body, they too will not last.
They will all swirl away, and I will be gone.
Yet nights still will pass and will turn into dawn.
There will be no more laughter. There will be no more jokes.
Just a silent, "That's all folks."

Debra...I was on a birding trip to Arizona in late April 2024, when I learned from a call from a birding stranger who had been staying with her that Debra, with whom I was going to visit and bird in Texas in a couple of days, had just died suddenly of a heart attack. Her death has affected me very deeply, the grieving being as close to my grieving for my mother as anything else that I have experienced.

But Then I Received the Call (4/26/24)

Debra Corpora, my friend. She is gone.
Beautiful person, forever is gone.
A birder, of course, together we'd roam.
Now I guess you could say that at last she's "gone home."
But her home was in Texas, in the Valley, on the coast,
In her beautiful gardens, a place she loved most.
So welcoming, so generous, my sweet birding friend.
A fighter for birds, for her health, to the end. RIP.

Lost (4/29/24)

Asleep, almost. Awaiting a plane,
Foggy, loopy, my tired old brain.
Drooping eyes, I'm not really here,
But lost in my memories of Debra, dear.

Debra (5/4/24)

There's nothing I can do for someone who has died.
The tears that I am crying, the many tears I've cried.
They will not bring her back.

Dogs

Soon after we married in 1968, my husband and I visited the local animal shelter in Anchorage and returned home with our first dog, Borea (think "boreal" or "Aurora borealis"). Although the Anchorage pound called her a "beagle mix," they were clueless. As best we could figure when she grew up, she was a whippet mix – a skinny black dog with small tipped-over ears, a white chest blaze and white feet. She lived for 17 years, a life that lasted that long in spite of her often munching on M&Ms, which in our ignorance we gave her as treats. Since then, we have almost always had a dog (or two, for a while). I rarely wrote about them until they were old and afflicted with something incurable, and I was dealing with letting go of them, and with their death.

Dying, and Our Dog Gale (6/2/98) Gale was our second dog, a shepherd/terrier mix with a beard and tufted elbows – very odd to behold but loving. We obtained her while living in Raleigh.

Been thinking about life, and all living things,
Particularly animals, including with wings.

The sickness of Gale, her terror, her pain
Has brought back with force, *her* ending, again.

The days when I saw her with fear in her eyes,
My mother, whose death, while not a surprise,

Brought me to feel that life's essence, the soul,
Goes on, is beyond, our grasp or control.

So dimly perceived in the eyes, in the stare,
In death there's a being escaping from there.

We so want to hold it, to see it, to know-
What happens at death? Where do we go?

Does our being burst forth? Is it good? Is there song?
Do we finally unite, after so very long?

Perhaps we're all captive, while we live here on earth,
In a particular body 'til death from our birth.

A time to connect to the beings we meet,
And then we pass on, a new passage, repeat.

A connection we feel between each separate soul,
A yearning for union, for knowing the whole.

I need to accept that there may always be
A barrier, an unknown, between you and me.

You, my good friend; you, my pet Gale,
I can't really know you. I try but I fail.

You'll finally escape with my longing unmet,
It's tormenting me, this longing, and yet,

It's better to love and to lose once again,
Than live without love, without friendship or friend.

Gale (7/25/98)

We did it; it's over; there's naught to be said,
Our darling sweet Gale has left us, is dead.

Charlie, Our Airedale (8/21/99) Charlie was our third dog, given to us by neighbors who decided they had too many dogs. He died suddenly of complications following torsion in the abdomen area, which can be fatal in large dogs and horses.

Charlie, our Charlie, the third of the three,
Beloved, and loving, canine trinity,

Huggable, fuzzy, devoted, our friend.
Close by us even to the swift bitter end,

If we sighed, he'd be worried; if we laughed, he'd rejoice,
Eyes glowing, tail wagging at the sound of our voice.

As we moved 'round the house, he'd be close by our side,
His loss leaves a chasm that cannot be denied.

I pray that whatever in dogs is the soul
Is somewhere, at peace, set free and made whole.

Ode to Caster (3/4/21) Caster is our current dog, the fifth, a husky mix obtained from a shelter in Anchorage, The shelter told us that he had been rounded up with other roaming dogs in a remote Alaskan village. They told us he was a "reactive rover," a way-too-accurate description. Caster does rhyme with "disaster." He moved with us to Wisconsin. He has adopted us fully, but his fierce, loud unwillingness to accept other people has limited our ability to travel and to have visitors.

It's dark. It's night. It's cold outside,
But lying hotly next to me-
"Reactive Rover" – he often is,
But now, he's as calm as he can be.

POEMS TO ORDER
(ON BEING ASKED TO WRITE POEMS)

I am not sure of the venue, but apparently, I took some sort of class or read a book in 2009, unremembered by me except for the output from it as we were asked to write poems, or write something, on a wide variety of topics, as follows.

LYNN E. BARBER

On being asked to write an "anti-love" poem (4/14/09)

She glared at him across the room, venom dripping from every pore.
What he'd done, she'd not forgive. This was it, the start of war.

There he sat, the clueless jerk, no idea of what he'd done,
But he would learn, oh yes, he would. Battle time had just begun.

She'd tell them all, she'd tell his friends, and they would learn each grim detail.
They'd turn away, leave him alone. It had to work. It could not fail.

So, she did it, and they did too. But did he notice? She'll never know.
Her anger beat her, felled her, sunk her, crushed her being from head to toe.

On being asked to write a "love poem" (4/14/09)

I've said that I love you so many times,
It sort of seems trite, like some of my rhymes.

But in fact, when I say it (and when I do not),
We both know it's there in each breath, in each thought.

It surrounds what we do, how we act, every day,
And is so much more than a thing that I say.

It is us, who we are, it is all we've been through,
But in case you forgot, let me say, "I love you!"

Thank you: On being asked to base a poem on a favorite poem (4/15/09) (a parody/take-off on ee cummings' poem)

Thank you dog for best an unfazing
Way: for the leaping wagging spirit of free
And a brown clown gleam of "wheee" and for everything
Which is joyful which is exuberant, which is "woof".

(dogs who have died still live today),

Making each day my birthday
A warm earth day of doggy treats,
And the soft fuzzy cuddly immeasurably soulful love

How should licking panting cavorting jumping
Rolling on dog-hairy floor
Do anything but cheer my human spirits

Be any better than unstoppable you
(now the ears of your ears are perked
And the heart of your heart is loving).

On being asked to write a poem with colors [maybe a haiku?] (4/16-19/09)

Green
Trees and grass
Come in so many hues,
Some so dark,
Others pale,
Pulsing, growing, chlorophyll.
Miracle of Life

On being asked to write a poem entitled "All I Want" (4/16-19/09)

All I want
Is to explain it
To tell you
(please listen)
I did not really mean it.
I am so sorry.
Do you hear?
I've tried very hard
But I can't
Seem to learn
What I need to do or say.
Please give me a hint.

On being asked to write an angry poem: Anger Control (4/16-19/09)

He'd written five books on anger control,
On keeping the peace, on saving your soul.

He believed every word; he'd worked himself through it.
He'd dealt with the worst; he knew how to do it.

Yet in spite of his knowledge, and in spite of his skill,
He had to admit that he knew he could kill

The woman who laughed and did not believe,
And said that his books were meant to deceive.

On being asked to write about an interaction in a particular specified poetic form (4/18/09)

The plunging hawk with talons spread,
The tiny sparrow far below
Darts in terror, filled with dread.
The plunging hawk with talons spread
Targets a squeaking mouse instead
Which has no clue on where to go.
The plunging hawk with talons spread
The tiny sparrow far below.

On being asked to write a work-related poem: My Boss (4/22/09)

I work for myself. I am such a good boss.
Of course, that means that for profit or loss,

I am solely responsible. There's no one but me
To service my clients, or those who would be.

But the good thing is that when I am tired,
My boss says, "Go rest," and I never get fired.

And when I want to go out and watch birds,
My boss says, "Be gone," without further words.

So, we go along, day after day,
Our lives inseparable. We go the same way.

On being asked to write about regret: Sorry (4/23/09)

I wish that I hadn't said it, although it was the truth.
It would have been excusable if I had been a youth.

But here I am a "senior". I surely should know better,
And if she wants to do it, I surely should have let her.

But I told her she was silly, without the brains God gave her,
And I regret sincerely my very poor behavior.

On being asked to write about an event (I chose the fourth of July, my husband David's birthday) (4/25/09)

The 4th of July
Is nearly nigh,
And so, I sigh.
It's David's day
(and the USA),
And so, I say,
It's time to pay
A visit to
A store or two –
A thing you do
When your love true
Is more than just 62.
We do not wait,
We celebrate.

On being asked to write about miscommunication (4/26/09)

There once was a girl who was clever,
But unbelievably, never
Were her words understood,
Though her diction was good,
And she made it her highest endeavor.

On being asked to write about longing (4/27/09)

Every Sunday I used to call my parents.
My mother would come to the phone,
And my father would feed her funny comments and questions that she would repeat to me.
I would update them on the past week of my life,
And they would tell me too—
Small things, little tidbits of living.
Nothing earth-shattering, but it made my world complete.
Now, when Sunday rolls around
Even though it's more than ten years ago,
I still want to hear their voices,
To be in their world,
And they in mine.
Sundays, our days together
Apart.

PANDEMIC POETRY

I did not write very many Covid-19 pandemic related poems, other than the first one below. The others below are related to our Anchorage Northern Lights Ringers handbell choir that kept practicing and playing outdoors during the pandemic. To cheer us all up, I wrote a few poems about ringing handbells through the pandemic.

Two Sicknesses (6/9/20)

The sicknesses deep, the sicknesses wide.
Deep within, and mostly denied.

One spread by virus, the other by hate.
How will we stop them? What is our fate?

Black lives do matter, as much as the "flu".
Pandemic distracts us. What can we do?

Masks on our faces, masks in our brains.
The former are helpful, the latter cause pains.

Our fears tend to swamp us, to make us withdraw.
Is caution a virtue, or deeply a flaw?

Let's pay attention, arise from our gloom –
Vanquish them both (perhaps using Zoom?).

Pandemic Bells (to a tune approximating "I'm Singing in the Rain") (9/17/20) Our outdoor rehearsals were outside, no matter the weather, where we played spaced 6 feet from each other.

We're ringing if it rains. We're ringing if it's not.
We ring our bells with joy, in weather cold or hot.
A smile behind each mask, there's nothing more we ask.
We're giving, we're giving, all we've got.

Snow Bells (to the tune of "Let It Snow") (10/14/20)

Oh, the weather out here is frightful, but the ringing's so delightful.
Since Caroline* won't let us go, let it snow, let it snow, let it snow.
Though our fingers will soon be numb, our bells joyful sounds will ring.

Through the weeks that will surely come, snow-muffled music we'll bring.
Oh, the weather out here is frightful, but the ringing's so delightful.
Our bells swinging to and fro, let it snow, let it snow, let it snow.
　*Caroline Valentine, our director

Northern Lights Ringers (tune: "Silver Bells") (12/24/20)

Where're we going? It is snowing! This must be a mistake.
I can't believe this is happening!
People freezing. People sneezing, bearing bells to the park.
It's Christmas Eve. What a lark!
Ringing bells, ringing bells. It's Christmas Eve and we're ringing.
Worshipping (worshipping), hear them ring (hear them ring).
Soon it will be Christmas Day.

Fiction/Stories

　I rarely knowingly write fiction in my poems, except in some of my childhood poems (above) but every now and then I've written little fictional oddities.

Accidental Stowaways (9/14/97) This poem is based on a real cricket that accompanied me on a weekend driving trip from Raleigh in a kayak on top of my car, across the water in a ferry to the Outer Banks and back again, and on a later Palm Warbler happening on a New Jersey pelagic birding trip.

It was just a little cricket. It chirped a little tune.
A cathedral in a kayak, under the summer moon.

I've heard a lot of crickets, and scarcely paused to note,
Until this chirping cricket, in a boat upon a boat.

I sort of started thinking, of meanings from the small,
But mostly, I forgot it, until a following fall.

It was just a little warbler, that landed on a boat,
I guess she thought it better than learning how to float.

I'd seen a million birds, and this was only one,
But this was something special, a spot of golden sun.

In fact, it brought the Son, or so it seemed to me,
A surprising source of grace, that showed me how to be.

Cricket Song (unknown date) This is a fictional account very loosely based on the same cricket story.

In a little town not far away,
Lived Sue and her brother Ray,
With their dad and mom, and their dog named Tom,
They were very happy both night and day.

Now Sue and Ray had a boat,
A little one, but it could float.
It was kept on the ground, with the grass growing 'round,
Its redness was something to note.

The boat was often alone,
So, a cricket made it his home.
He lived way inside, in a place where he'd hide,
Like a king on his own little throne.

In the evenings the cricket would sing.
He began each year in the spring.
A cathedral he had; it made his heart glad,
With his voice through the boat echoing.

Now Sue and Ray went one day,
To the ocean – quite far away.
They took along their boat, the one that could float.
For they intended to play.

For hours, the boat sat there,
Perched so high in the air.
They played on the land, the grass and the sand,
And the cricket just chirped in despair.

A couple of days passed this way,
And the cricket grew hotter each day,
Neither Sue nor Ray knew, what the cricket went through,
They were much too busy at play.

Robin Plates – Imagining (~3/20/21) When I heard in the news about a woman giving away some plates, I began to wonder about the plates and imagined one, decorated with a robin painting, that did not get given away…

I read about the woman who gave away plates.
To her they were sentient, aware and alive.
She said there were four, but in fact there were not.
In fact, there were more. In fact, there were five.

Away in a corner removed from the four
Was another, a chipped one, forlorn and unsought,
Unwanted, discarded, unmatched and alone,
I sat out of sight, not given a thought.

Once again, it was quiet. No one answered my calls.
The chatterers, silenced, away.
What was an ancient old robin to do?
Who would I talk to? With whom would I play?

My family, once numerous, now broken and gone
Had once filled the cupboard with robinesque song.
Someday I will see them, whole and restored,
For now, I will wait, I am sure, not for long.

Jack and Jill (12/26/22)

This poem came from some unknown place, even before I was writing my book-in-progress about owls.

Jack and Jill went up the hill
To fetch a pail of water.
Jack fell down and broke his crown,
And Jill came tumbling after.

What occurred? It was absurd.
It was fair and it was foul.
The scary sight that starry night?
They heard and saw a Great Horned Owl!

VERY MISCELLANEOUS

Look at the Two of Them! (6/24/24)
Some thoughts on hearing the nightly news.

Enough of this age thing! Look at these men!
Look at them now; look at them then.
Look at their morals, their hours and their lives.
Look at how they've treated their wives.
See what they've done. See how they've led.
Hear what they're saying, and what they have said.
Look at our land with each man at the helm.
Look – but don't let the facts overwhelm.
Now we must speak so that others will hear.
And of course, we must vote – out of hope (and of fear).

Lemmings – Read It and Weep (11/08/24, three days after we voted)

Like lemmings they run, being led from behind.
None of them really seeming to mind
That down in the waters churning below
Lie demons and sorrows (really, they know!).
But nothing can stop their inevitable plunge
As blindly, unheeding they forwardly lunge.
On the sidelines we watch with terror and grief
And pray that somehow there will be a relief,
That blind eyes will see, that hatred and fear
Will be turned into caring as year turns to year.

Phrazle (10/9/23) Most people have heard of Wordle, but fewer know about Phrazle. I love Phrazle, and every time I figure out another of its phrases, I want to write a story with as many as possible phrases in it of those that have been in Phrazle. For now, I need to be satisfied with this little poem, which has at least eleven well-known phrases in it.

Take the red-eye, she said with a sigh,
You know you are the apple of my eye.
You must seize the day, and not hit the hay,
Fish or cut bait, or you'll rue it someday.
A little bird told me, it's not my cup of tea,
A rain check I'll take; it's better for me.
In layman's terms, I'll stay in the dark.
I know it's not a walk in the park.
Though I'll turn on a dime, I don't have the time
To waste more energy on this little rhyme.

More Phrazle (7/18/24)

"A little bird told me" -- the Phrazle of the day.
It has to start a poem (but I don't know what to say).

And More – 17 Recent Phrazle Phrases (8/7/24)

It was the bane of my existence, a bridge too far.
I ought to have known not to reach for a star.
Beyond the pale, a kangaroo court,
A hard nut to crack, selling up short.
All in all, I am now back to square one.
I'll nip it in the bud, second to none.
With my head above water, with the upper hand,
Taking the edge off, taking a stand,
In one fell swoop, I'm now on a roll,
Back in the saddle – a heart and a soul.

**… Of course, I will continue to "waste time" on birding
and on rhyming (and on Phrazle).
And sometimes I can figure out what to say.**

INDEX

Please note: most names of bird species in this Index are alphabetized by the common name (by the first word of the full common name if the name in the text has multiple words) and that people are mostly alphabetized by first name.

A Charisma of Owls, 3
ABA Area, 113, 114, *138*
ABA big year, 2, *53*, *58*, *127*, *128*, 138, *139*, *141*, *149*
ACLU, *2*, *166*
Adak, *66*, *67*, *144*
Air-eaters, 31
AK big year, 3
Alabama, 88
Alaska, *4*, *8*, *12*, *13*, 37, *61*, 65, 71, 88, *102*, 127, *129*, 138, 144, *145*, 152, *153*, *166*, *194*, 222, 224, 225
Alaska National Wildlife Refuge, *144*
Alaska's North Slope, *144*
Albatross, *99*, *104*
Alcan, *11*
American Birding Association, 54, *149*
American Goldfinch, *85*
American Woodcock, 28
Anahuac National Wildlife Refuge, *56*
Anchorage, *3*, *8*, *12*, *13*, 65, *162*, *164*, *166*, *193*, *222*, *247*, *249*, *254*
Anchorage Audubon Society, *166*
Anna's Hummingbird, *162*, *164*

Annie, 243, 244
Antarctica, *98*, 123
Antbird, 121
Antwren, *121*
Anwar (ANWR), *144*
Apo Sunbird, 109
Aracari, 121
Argentina, *98*
Arizona, *84*, *113*, *138*, *245*, *246*
Attu, 63
Attu, AK, *61*
Audubon, *2*
Audubon's Shearwater, 124
Australia, 89
Babbler, *94*, 106, 108, 119
Bachman's Sparrow, 51
Bacteriology, *2*, 183
Baird's Sparrow, *115*
Bald Head Island, *50*
Baltimore Oriole, 32, *85*
Barbet, 94
Barred Owl, *85*
Beagle, *100*
Ben King, *92*, *106*
Bhutan, *92*, *93*, *94*, *95*, *96*, *97*
Big year, 3, 12, 39, 53, 54, 57, 77, 91, 125, 126, 127, 128, 129, 130, 133, 134, 136, 137, 138, 139, 142, 143, 145, 149, 150, 151, 153, 155, 156, 159

Big Years, Biggest States: Birding in Texas and Alaska, *3*
Bird lists, *23, 36, 88*
Birds in Trouble, 3
Black Mountain, 167
Blackbird, *67, 69, 86, 114*
Black-capped Chickadee, *20, 25*
Black-necked Crane, *119*
Black-necked Stilt, *86*
Blue Bunting, *150*
Blue Jay, 18, 36, *68, 233*
Bluebird, 46
Bluethroat, *104*
Boca Manu, *112*
Bohol, *108*
Booby, *51*
Boot Springs, 138
Borea, *247*
Bowl, the, *126*
Bridled Tern, *124*, 125
Brown Thrasher, *22*
Brown, Charles, *181*
Bufflehead, *51, 83*
Bulbul, 94, 108
Bull Junior Creek, *5, 30, 33*
Bunny, *70*
Bunting, 94, *105, 150*
Bush Chat, *96*
Buzzard, *104*
Caimen, 113
California, *113, 138*
Cally, 193
Canada, 3, 13, 37, 53, 127, 138
Canvasback, *51*
Caracas, *90*
Cardinal, *77, 86*, 228
Carolina Bird Club, *2, 50, 166*
Caroline, 255, 256

Caster, *249*
Cat, 84
Catbird, 14, 36
Cebu, *108*
Cetti's Warbler, *104*
Charlie, *248*
Chasing, *154, 156, 157*
Chestnut-sided Warbler, *75*
Chickadee, *18, 67, 70, 145*
Chicken, *4, 5, 6, 7, 16, 27*
Chiffchaff, *105*
Chile, 89
Chipping Sparrow, *14*, 32, *158*
Chocolate, *71, 118*
Christmas Day, *52, 136, 256*
Church, 45, 75, 166, 174, 176, 222
Church pastor, *10, 193*
Classic, *59*
Clay-colored Sparrow, *32*
Cock-of-the Rock, *112*
Common Crane, *141*
Common Gallinule, *55*
Common Myna, *149*
Community United Church of Christ, *2, 191*
Computer, *198*
Coot, 51, 101
Corvallis, *2, 4, 9, 89, 193, 194*
Corvus, *29, 30*
Cory's Shearwater, 124
Costa Rica, *2, 89, 90*
Coucal, 108
Covid, *13, 222, 254*
Crag Martin, *118*
Crane, 36, *51, 64, 65, 68, 81*, 86, *101*, 116, *118, 119, 141, 142, 153*
Creeper, *121*
Crex, 101

Cricket, *256, 257*
Crimson-collared Grosbeak, *150*
Crow, 7, *29, 30, 52, 68*, 83, *86*, 94, *105*, 154, *233*
Cuba, *115*
Cuckoo-dove, *106*
Cuckoo-shrike, *106*
Curlew, 62
Cuzco, 112
D.C. Everest High School, Schofield, 1
Dabbler, 67
Daddy, 3, 14, 24, 235, 237, 240, 241, 243
Dark-eyed Juncos, *31*
Dave, *1, 2, 3, 8, 10, 13, 74, 92, 132, 174, 191, 192, 193, 194, 195, 212, 220, 222, 242*
Death, *228, 233, 238, 239*
Debra, 246
Dipper, *94, 119*
Disko, *98*
Dog, 84
Dove, 48
Downy Woodpecker, 34
Drake Passage, *98*
Drongo, *94, 108*
Druk-trucks, *97*
Dry Tortugas, *123*
Duck, *3, 7, 14, 51, 67, 72, 101, 115*
Duke University, *2*, 186
Durham, *2*
Dusky Thrush, 63
dying, 229, 230
Dying, 228, 247
Eagle, 112, 153
Eastern Kingbird, *28, 32*
Eastern Meadowlark, 24

Eastern Screech-Owl, *85*
Eau de Deet, *57*
eBird, *38*
Ecuador, *120*
ee cummings, 204, 250
Egret, *51*
Eider,, 153
Ellen and Fred, 226
England, 89
Euphonia, 112
Extreme Birder: One Woman's Big Year, *2, 39*
CLAY, *174*
Fantail, 109
Far Eastern Curlew, 63
Ferruginous Flycatcher, *118, 119*
Field Guides, *120, 121*
Finch, 105
Finland, *101, 102, 103*
Firethroat, *118, 119*
First Congregational UCC, *2*, 222
Flamingo, *148*
Flicker, 34, *116*
Florida, *148*
Flowerpecker, 106, 108, 109
Flycatcher, *51*, 76, *121*
Forktail, *94*
Fort Caswell, *50*
Fort Fisher, *50*
Fort Worth, *2, 4, 10, 11, 12, 33, 58, 160, 166, 214, 221*
Fort Worth Audubon, 166
Frigatebird, *125*
Fruit-Dove, 108
Fulvetta, *94, 118*
Furtive Flycatcher, *107*
Galapagos Islands, *91*
Gale, *247, 248*

Galliformes, 117
Gambell, *152*
Gannet, *51*
Georgia, 142
Gleaner, *121*
Gnatcatcher, *114*
Goldfinch, *19*, 36, *52*, *76*, *85*
Google map app, *73*
Gooney bird, 104
Goose, 7, 52, 69, 72, 81, 152
Grackle, *30*, *31*
Gray Bush Chat, *96*
Gray-headed Chickadee, *102*, *145*
Great Crested Flycatcher, *32*
Great Horned Owl, *85*, *259*
Great Texas Birding Classic, *59*
Greater Prairie-Chicken, *27*
Grebe, *101*
Green-breasted Mango, *142*
Grosbeak, *150*
Ground tit, *116*
Grouse, 51
Gruidae, 119
Guadalupe Mountains, *126*
Gulf Shores, Alabama, *36*
Gulf., 138
Gull, 64, 82
Gyrfalcon, 152
Hairy Woodpecker, 34
Handbell, 256
Handbell, 254, 255
Hanging-parrots, *106*
Harpy Eagle, *107*
Hawk, 82, *115*
Hawk-cuckoo, 108
Henlow's Sparrow, 51
Hermit Warbler, 59
Hidden Brain, *79*

Holy Land, *104*
Honduras, *122*
Hooded Sunbird, 109
Hoopoe, *105*
Horicon Marsh, *77*, *86*
Human Rights, 2
Humm, *161*, *162*, *164*
Hummingbird, *11*, *138*, *142*, 160, *161*, *162*, *164*, *165*
Ibis, 109
Icebergs, *99*, *153*
India, 92
Israel, *104*, *105*
Ivory Gulls, *153*
Jaeger, 103, *126*
Jay, 164
JD degree, 2
Jeepney, *110*, *111*
Jordan, *104*
Jynx, 102
Kenya, *91*
Kingbird, *28*, *30*
KingBird Tours, *39*, *92*, *93*, *105*, *116*
Kinglet, 152
Kite, *104*, 108, *119*
Lammergeier, *118*
Lark, *66*, *101*, *104*, *115*, *118*, *152*, *179*
Laughing Gull, 125
Laughingthrush, *94*, 97, 119
Law career, *186*
Law degree, *9*, *10*
Law school, 2
Laysan Albatross, *104*
LBJs, *32*
LeConte's Thrasher, *114*
Lemmings, 260
Lena, *112*
Life list, 113

Lima, 113
Limpkin, *77, 86*
Linda Ferraresso, 61
Little Owl, *104*
Little Stint, 66
Loja Hummingbird, 121
Long-Eared Owl, 83
Lower Rio Grande Valley, *53*
Luzon, *106, 107*
Macaw, *113*
Machu Pichu, 113
Madison, 1, *2, 8, 11, 13*, 193, *194*
Madison Arboretum, *8*
Magpie, *94, 164*
Mallard, *48*
Mama, 25, 230, 231, 234, 235, 239, 243
Mangrove Flycatcher, *108*
Manteo, 49
Marathon County, 3, *4, 5, 24, 34*
Marsh Wren, *86*
Masked Booby, *124*
Masked Duck, *59*
Massachusetts Audubon Society, *90, 98*, 104
McGregor's Cuckoo-Shrike, 109
MDiv degree, *2, 10*
Meadowlark, *14, 21, 23, 24, 70, 115*
Melodious Babbler, *107*
Merchant's Mill Pond, *52*
Meteorology, *1, 2, 8, 9, 11, 12, 191*
Meteorology professor, *2*
Mew Gulls, *65*
Mexico, *2*
Microbiology, *8, 9, 183*

Midway Island, *104*
Mindanao, *109*
Minia, *94*
Minivet, *94*, 97
Mink, *3, 5, 7, 24, 25, 29, 30*
Mississippi Kite, *51*
Monal, *116*
Moorhen, *54, 55*
Morning pages, *195*
Mosinee, *1, 4, 5, 7, 20, 22, 27, 234*
Mosquito,, 50
Mosquitos, *57*
Mother, 2, 6, 14, 20, 26, 35, 36, 48, 73, 74, 228, 229, 234, 238, 245, 246, 247, 254
Mourning Dove, 85
Murre, 64
Murrelet Manor, 61
Murrelettes, 61
Myna, *94*, 109, *148*
Namekagon Barrens Wildlife Area, *155*
Naomi, *73*
Naumann's Thrush, *66*
NC, *49*
NCSU, *2, 9*
Nebraska, 141
Negros Island, *108*
New Jersey, *122, 256*
Nitrogen-fixing, 9
Nome, *65, 66*
North Carolina, *2, 50, 52, 112, 167*
North Carolina, *4*
North Carolina, *9*
North Carolina, *11*
North Carolina, *45*
North Carolina, *50*
North Carolina, *50*

North Carolina, *50*
North Carolina, *112*
North Carolina, *166*
North Carolina, *166*
North Carolina, *196*
North Carolina, *228*
North Carolina Human Rights Coalition, *166*
North Carolina State University, *9*
Northern Bobwhite, *27*
Northern Cardinal, *85*
Northern Hills Bird Club, *166*
Northern Lights Ringers, 254
NPR, *79*
Nuthatch, 126
Obmascik, *138*
Obsession, *46, 78, 81, 148, 158, 159, 207*
Ohio, 193
Oklahoma, *60*
Olive & Olive, *2*
Oregon, *4, 9, 11, 194*
Oregon State University, *9*
Oriole, 30, 32, 52, 59, 158
Outer Banks, *256*
Ovenbird, *25, 26, 52*
Overton, *124*
Owl, *3, 46, 51, 59, 61, 79, 83, 84, 85, 86, 93, 101, 106, 117, 152, 153, 259*
Palm Warbler, 256
Panda, *116*
Pandemic, *13, 222, 254*
Panhandle, *53*
Parakeet, 121
Parent, *4, 5, 6, 7, 22, 23, 24, 29, 33, 35, 74, 228, 244, 254*
Partridge, *94, 116,* 117
Parula, *52*

Patent attorney, *2, 9, 10*
Patent law, 2, 9
Pea Island, 49, *51*
Peep, 50, *51,* 59
Pelagic, *51, 122, 124, 125, 126, 127, 138, 146, 256*
Penguin, *98, 100, 123*
Peru, *112*
Pet shop, *15, 16*
Petrel, *99*
Pewee, *67, 76,* 158
Pheasant, *27, 46, 116,* 117, 119
Phenology list, 36
Philippine Hawk-Eagle, *106*
Philippine Islands, *105,* 111
Phrazle, 260, 261
Piculet, *121*
Piedmont, *51*
Pigeon, *25, 94*
Pileated Woodpecker, *34*
Pineywoods, *53*
Pipit, *63, 104, 115,* 152
Pitta, 108
Plover, *51*
Polyphemus moth, *31*
Poor People's Campaign, *166, 173*
Prairie-Chicken, 27, 36
Prasad, *125*
Prions, *99*
Prohaska, 36
Puffin, 64
Pygmy Nuthatch, *126*
Quail, *27, 114, 115*
Racquet-tail, 109
Rail, 56, 59, 75, 101, 115
Raleigh, *2, 4, 9, 10,* 89, *173, 194, 206, 212, 234, 245, 247, 256*
Rapid City, *2, 4, 12, 221*

Raptor, *104*, *106*, 114, *238*
Raven, *154*
RBA, *52*
Recordkeeping, *37*
Red-bellied Woodpecker, 34
Red-cockaded Woodpecker, *51*
Red-eyed Vireo, *75*, *76*, 158
Red-headed Woodpecker, 34
Red-necked Phalarope, 125
Redpoll, 152
Redshank, *102*
Redstart, *76*, *119*
Red-winged Blackbird, 86
Reeve Airlines, *63*
Research Microbiologist, *2*
Research Triangle Park, *9*
Rhizobium, *9*
Ring-necked Pheasant, *27*
Robin, *14*, *25*, *33*, *36*, *37*, *77*, *94*, *117*, *258*
Rock Pigeon, 24
Rockport, *151*, *219*
Rook, *101*
Rosefinch, *117*
Ross's Goose, *72*
Rosy-finch, 157
Ruff, 64, *101*, *103*
Ruffed Grouse, *27*
Rufie, *160*, *161*
Rufous Hummingbird, 160
Ruth, *73*
Sabine Woods, *56*
Sage-grouse, 27
Saker, 116
Sandgrouse, *104*
Sandhill Crane, 36, 77, 86, 141
Sandpiper, 49
Saw-whet Owl, *76*
Scarlet (and George), *136*
Schofield, 1, *3*, *4*, *5*

Scissor-tailed Flycatcher, *33*, *34*, 60
Scoter, *57*
Seed snipe, *121*
Shama, 106
Shar, *151*, *220*
Sharp-tailed Grouse, *156*
Shearwater, *51*, *124*
Shorebird, 50, 62, 67, 102, 103
Shortwing, 106
Shoveler, *51*
Siberian Tit, *102*, *145*
Sichuan, *116*, *119*
Simon Perkins, 90, 98, 101
Siskin, *83*, *101*
Sister, 3, 5, 7, 24, 74, 89
Skylark, *116*
Smew, *66*, *102*, *103*
Smooth-billed Ani, *148*
Snipe, 28, 101
Snow Bunting, *135*, *136*
Snow Geese, *51*
Snowcock, 118
Snowy Owl, *36*, *81*, *82*, *152*, *153*
Solo Law Practice, *188*, *189*
Song Sparrow, 85
Sooty Tern, 124
South America, *98*
South Dakota, *12*, *127*, *128*, *129*, *155*, *166*, *220*
South Dakota Ornithologists Union, *166*
South Padre Island, *135*
South Rice Lake, *71*
Sparrow, *32*, *48*, *51*, *59*, *114*
Spectacled Owl, 90
Spruce Grouse, *80*, *81*
Squirrel, *7*, *19*, *82*
St. David, *132*

St. Paul Island, *64*
Starling, *7, 24, 83*
Sternberg, *3, 4*
Stone-Curlew, *104*
Stork, 105
Storm-Petrel, *124*
Sunbird, 106
Sunbird Tours, 91
Susan, *76*
Swainson's Warbler, 51
Swallow, 85, 119
Swamp Sparrow, 158
Swan, *72, 81, 101, 103, 150*
Swift, 21, *101, 104, 119*
Swordbill, *121*
Sylph, *121*
Tanager, *112*, 121
Tapaculo, *121*
Tern, 64, 103, 124
Texas, *2, 3, 10, 11, 28, 33, 53, 56, 57, 59, 61, 124, 126, 127, 128, 129, 130, 132, 133, 135, 139, 166, 195, 220, 246*
Texas A&M University Press, *2*, 220
Texas Ornithological Society, 56, *166*, 220
The Big Year, *128, 138*
the Valley, 138
Thick-billed Kingbird, *135*
Thrasher, 30, 31, 66, 74, 113, *114*
Thrush, *62, 67, 101, 116, 179*
Ticks, *50*
Tit, 116
Titmouse, 126
Tody, *116*
Tok, 67
Tony, *59*
Toucan, *121*

Towhee, *114*
Tragopan, 94
Trogon, *94, 108, 116, 121*
Tropicbird, *51, 124, 125*
Tufted Flycatcher, *60*
Tundra Swan, *51*
TX big year, 2, 3
Tyrannulet, *121*
UNA, *167, 168*
Unconvention, 80
United Church of Christ, *174, 191*
United Nations Association, *166, 167*
University of Wisconsin, 8
US Weather Service, *2, 8*
USDA, 2, *9*
Veery, 77
Venezuela, *90*
Vulture, 48, 58
Wagtail, *63, 104, 118, 119*
Wake Audubon, *166*
Warbler, *21, 26, 46, 50, 51, 52, 59, 67, 69, 116, 118, 119*
Warbling Vireo, 158
Washington, D.C., 168
Wattled Broadbill, *111, 112*
Wausau, *1*, 3, 4, 13, 67, 75, 77, 166, 226
Wausau Bird Club, 75, *166*
Waxwing, *83*
Weather Bureau, *8*
Western Meadowlark, 24
Whale, 124
Wheatears, *104*
Whip-poor-will, 28
White-eye, 108, 109
Whitethroat, *105*
White-winged Cuckoo Shrike, *108*

269

Whooper Swan, *150*
Whooping Crane, 86
WI big year, 3
Wide-billed Sandpiper, *103*
Wilderness Birding Adventures, *66, 152*
Wilson's Snipe, *28*
Wings Birding Tours, 113
Winnie, 57
Wisconsin, *3, 4, 5, 7, 8, 13, 20, 22, 25, 34, 35, 36, 39, 53, 67, 71, 77, 79, 80, 86, 88, 127, 129, 153, 155, 166, 193, 194, 204, 222, 224, 225, 226, 228, 241, 249*
Wisconsin Public Radio, 39

Wisconsin Society for Ornithology, *3, 79, 80, 166*
Wolong, *116, 119*
Woodcock, 28
Woodpecker, *34, 101*, 118
Wren, *52, 77, 85, 112*, 153
Wryneck, *102, 104*
WSO, *79, 82*
Yak, *117*
Yard, 5, 6, 10, 12, 28, 29, 33, 53, 61, 83, 162, 221
Yellow-bellied Sapsucker, 34
Yellow-billed Loon, *103*
Yellow-headed Blackbird, 86
Yellow-rumped Warbler, *51*
Zoology, *1, 8*

www.ingramcontent.com/pod-product-compliance
Lightning Source LLC
LaVergne TN
LVHW042250070526
838201LV00089B/100